New National Curriculum Edition

INTO GEOGRAPHY

BOOK 4

Patricia Harrison   Steve Harrison   Mike Pearson

Nelson

Acknowledgements

Mr and Mrs Ashworth
Butlin's Ltd
Don Cook and the pupils of Conniburrow Middle School, Milton Keynes
Linda Edmondson
The Royal Geographical Society
The Ghariwallah family, India
Gwynedd Council/Cyngor Sir
Milton Keynes Development Corporation
James Price
David Shepherd
Brian Smith, Norwich City Planning Officer
John Townson, Brookhouse farm
The Ordnance Survey

Photographs by Aerofilms Ltd (pp. 4, 48), Elizabeth Pearson (pp. 8, 9, 11, 49, 61), Barratt (p. 9), Geonex (p. 19), Zefa (p. 21), Wellington International Services (pp. 22, 23), Steve Harrison (pp. 32, 35, 36, 50, 51), The Image Bank (p. 49), Shell (pp. 57, 58), Peter Menzel, Science Photo Library (p. 61), Mark Edwards/Still Pictures (p. 63)

Cover photograph by the Image Bank

Original design by Barrie Richardson

Illustrated by Terry Bambrook, Ray Mutimer, PFP Art and Type Ltd, John Plumb, Barrie Richardson, Colin Smithson and Taurus Graphics

The publishers have made every attempt to trace copyright holders of reprinted material, and apologise for any errors or omissions.

Thomas Nelson and Sons Ltd
Nelson House Mayfield Road
Walton-on-Thames Surrey
KT12 5PL UK

51 York Place
Edinburgh
EH1 3JD UK

Thomas Nelson (Hong Kong) Ltd
Toppan Building 10/F
22A Westlands Road
Quarry Bay Hong Kong

Thomas Nelson Australia
102 Dodds Street
South Melbourne
Victoria 3205 Australia

Nelson Canada
1120 Birchmount Road
Scarborough Ontario
M1K 5G4 Canada

© Patricia Harrison, Steve Harrison, Mike Pearson 1989, 1993

First published by E J Arnold and Son Ltd 1989
ISBN 0-560-66711-6

This fully revised edition published by Thomas Nelson and Sons Ltd 1993
ISBN 0-17-425054-1
NPN 9 8 7 6 5 4 3 2

All rights reserved. No paragraph of this publication may be reproduced, copied or transmitted save with written permission or in accordance with the provisions of the Copyright, Design and Patents Act 1988, or under the terms of any licence permitting limited copying issued by the Copyright Licensing Agency, 90 Tottenham Court Road, London W1P 9HE.

Any person who does any unauthorised act in relation to this publication may be liable to criminal prosecution and civil claims for damages.

Printed in Great Britain.

CONTENTS

Exploring a City Centre	4
Inner City	6
Urban Renewal	8
New Towns	10
Milton Keynes: Location	12
Milton Keynes: Networks	14
Getting to Dover	16
Dover	18
Calais	20
Calais: A Tourist Town	22
Latitude and Longitude	24
Latitude and Longitude	26
Time Zones	28
India: Urban and Rural	30
India: Families and Change	32
India: Success and Failure	34
A Future in the City	36
Ups and Downs	38
Contours Down	40
Contours Up	42
Weather and Climate	44
Weather and Climate	46
Rivers in Flood	48
North Wales: Fieldwork	50
North Wales: Farming	52
Nuclear Shock	54
Oil and Gas	56
On a Rig	58
Using Oil and Gas	59
Volcanoes and Earthquakes	60
Checkpoint: The World	62
A Greener World Game	64

EXPLORING A CITY CENTRE

City centres are exciting places. They have shops, museums, factories, multi-storey car parks, bus and railway stations. Sally and David are visiting Norwich. While there, they hope to visit four places: the Castle Museum, the Cathedral, the market, and a famous medieval street called Elm Hill.

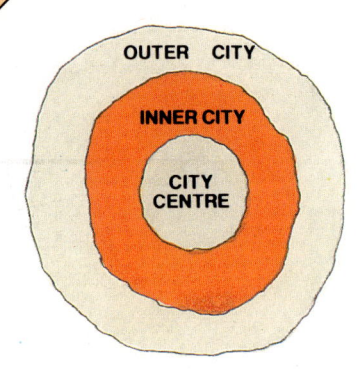

Assignment A

Compare the aerial photograph and the map of central Norwich.

1 a) Does the map or the aerial photograph tell you about the height of buildings?

b) How many storeys high is City Hall?

2 a) Older buildings are made of flint, limestone and old brick. Which shows this best, the photograph or the map?

b) What are newer buildings made of?

3 Which season of the year was the photograph taken? Give a reason for your answer.

4 Write two sentences describing what sort of place Norwich looks like from the aerial photograph.

5 a) How many old churches can you see on the photograph?

b) How many are shown on the map?

c) How can you tell the difference on the photograph between the Cathedral and the churches?

6 Which is most help to Sally and David for exploring Norwich, the aerial photograph or the map? Explain why.

One step further

Imagine friends from another area are coming to stay at your home, and you are going to show them around your local town or city centre.

a) Draw a sketch map from memory of your town centre showing five interesting places to visit. These can be buildings or spaces like parks.

b) Draw a key to explain your map.

c) Add more details to your map such as names of important roads, shop names, car parks, bus and railway stations.

d) Describe why the five places you have chosen would interest visitors.

Key to some of Norwich's churches and church buildings

1. Cathedral
   1A Erpingham Gate
   1B St Ethelberts Gate and Chapel
2. St Peter Mancroft
3. St Andrews
4. St Andrews Hall (now a concert hall)
5. Blackfriars Hall (now a public hall)
6. St Michael at Pleas (now an exhibition centre)
7. St Peter Hungate (now a museum)
8. St Simon and St Jude (now a scout headquarters)
9. St George Tombland
10. St John Maddermarket (now a Greek Orthodox Church)

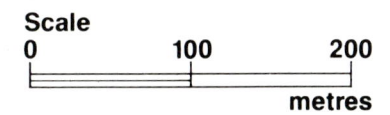

Scale: 0 — 100 — 200 metres

It is useful to locate a place on a map by giving the four figure grid reference. For example on the map of Central Norwich, the grid reference of Timberhill is (13,21).

KEY

- mostly shops and services
- mostly offices
- factories and warehouses
- important public buildings
- churches
- colleges and schools
- houses
- grass, trees, open spaces
- roads, car parks

Assignment B

Using the map of Central Norwich:

1. Give the grid references for
   a) the Market Place
   b) Shire Hall
   c) Elm Hill
   d) Back of the Inns

2. What important buildings are in
   a) (11,26) b) (12,22)
   c) (10,22)

3. Work out a route Sally and David can follow to see the four places they wish to visit. List the streets in order along the route and the places to be seen on the way. Start and finish at City Hall Car Park (10,20).

4. Use the scale to estimate how many kilometres and metres Sally and David have to walk.

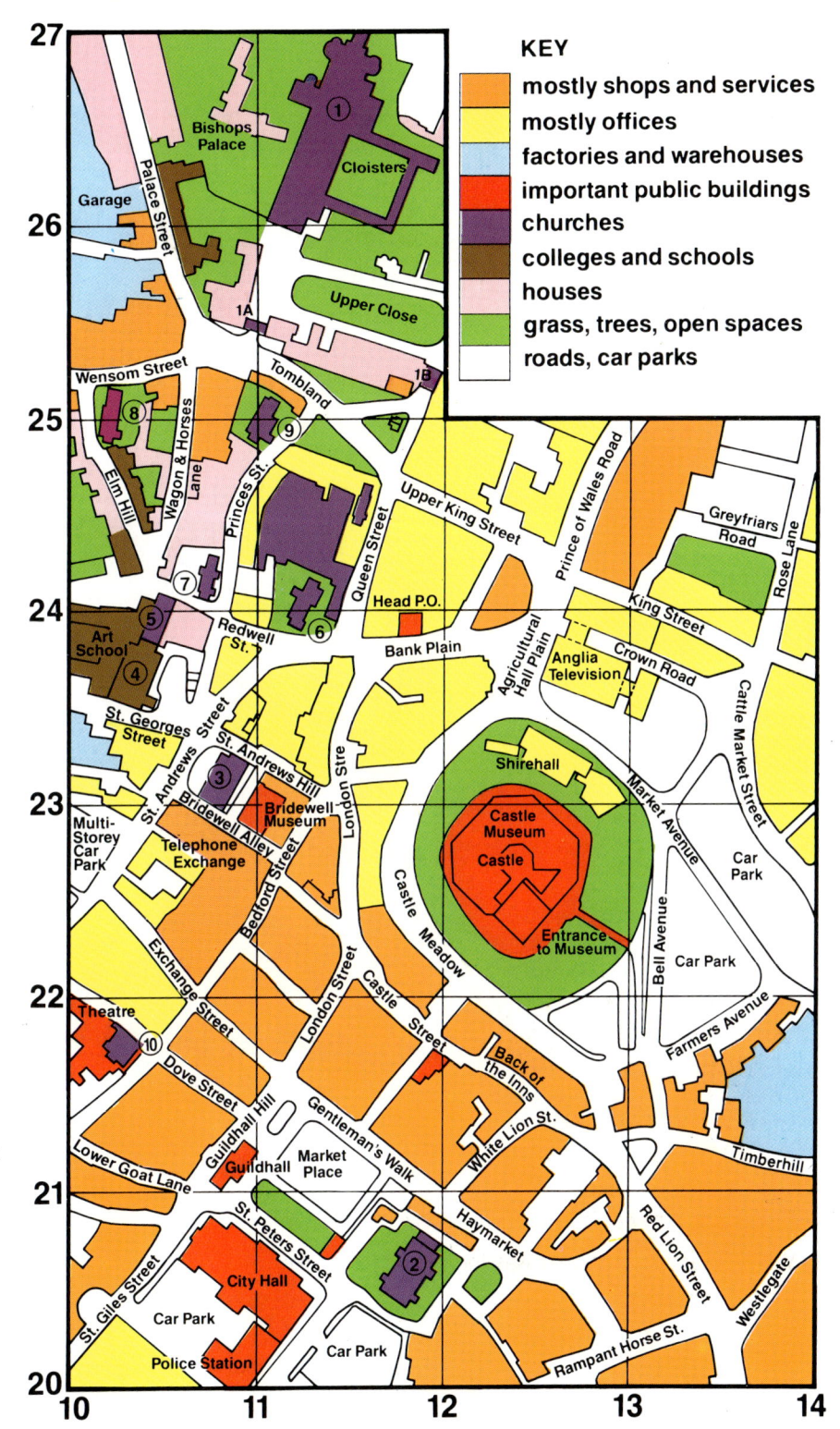

5. What activities might have taken place in
   a) Weavers Lane b) Haymarket c) Tombland?

6. Name three buildings which have changed their use. How are they used today?

INNER CITY

MAP A   Land use in Grotton, 1950

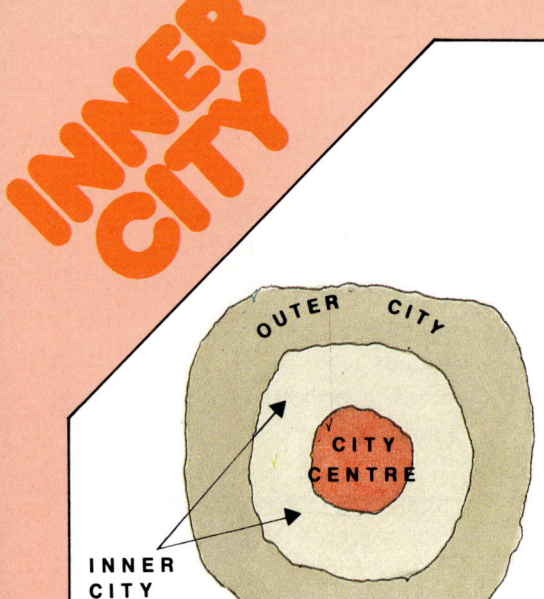

Near the centres of most old industrial towns are areas with many old houses and some newer houses and flats. The old houses are often in a poor state of repair.

Usually this part of the town has factories, warehouses and old schools. Parks are few and far between. We call such an area the **inner city**.

Sometimes the inner city has land with heaps of rubble where houses and factories have been pulled down (demolished). We call these untidy areas **derelict land**.

Map A shows how the land was used in Grotton Inner City in 1950. We call this a **land use map**. Map B shows the same area today.

Assignment

Compare map A with map B.

Complete the table to show the changes which have taken place.

	Grid reference	Land uses in 1950	Land uses today
a)	(30,50)		
b)		Cinema	
c)	(33,52)		
d)			Polytechnic
e)	(33,53)		
f)	(33,50)		

MAP B Land use in Grotton today

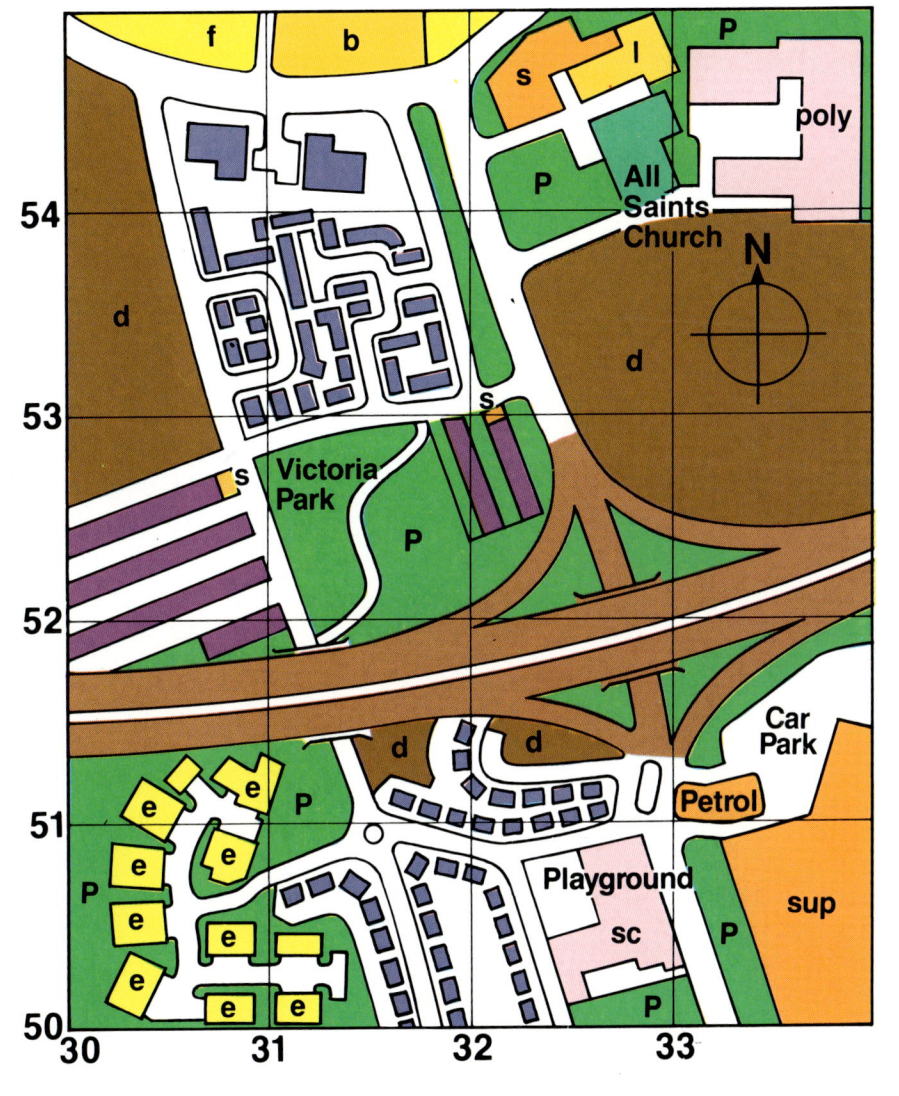

Personal Research

1. Talk with some older people to find out how the town centre and the area around it have changed in their lifetime. Ask questions about changes in shopping, housing, entertainment and transport.

2. Look at a large scale Ordnance Survey map of your town centre (1:1250 scale). What date was the map printed? Discuss with your friends any changes in the centre since the map was published. Are the changes an improvement or not?

3. Describe an area of your town centre which looks shabby, rundown or derelict. Is anyone doing anything about it? Talk with your friends and make a list of possible improvements. Draw pictures and plans of the town centre you would like to see.

4. Make a simple land use map of a small area near your school or near your home.

Key for maps A and B

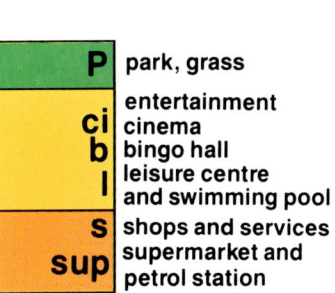

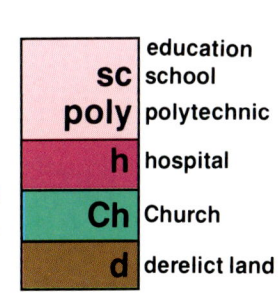

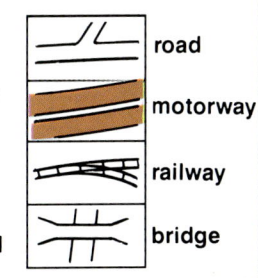

- old houses
- new flats and houses
- **f** industrial areas / factories and warehouses
- **st** steelworks
- **c** coalmine
- **e** new industrial estate
- **P** park, grass
- **ci** entertainment cinema
- **b** bingo hall
- **l** leisure centre and swimming pool
- **s** shops and services
- **sup** supermarket and petrol station
- **sc** education school
- **poly** polytechnic
- **h** hospital
- **Ch** Church
- **d** derelict land
- road
- motorway
- railway
- bridge

One step further

1. Why is the supermarket and petrol station in a good position?
2. Give the grid references and names of two places which have not changed.
3. Are there more or fewer corner shops today than in 1950? Give reasons for your answer.
4. Which do you think are the three most important changes in this inner city area?

URBAN RENEWAL

Major changes are taking place to houses and the environment in the inner city.

The work is called **urban renewal**.

Photo A shows Dallas Street, where Sajid's grandparents live, when the council workers started the improvements. Photo B shows Dallas Street after improvement.

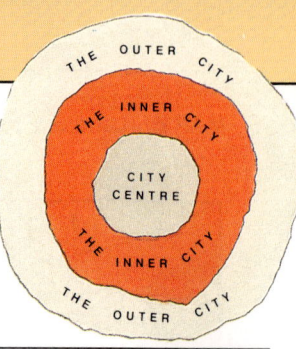

A

B

Assignment A

1. What complaints do you think Dallas Street people made at the time photo A was taken?
2. Why were there no garages when these terraced houses were built in the 1890s?
3. Why does a lack of garages make it difficult for car owners living in the inner city today?
4. How has parking been made better in Dallas Street?
5. Dallas Street is now 'one-way only' for traffic. Why is this an improvement?
6. How has the surface of the street corner been made more interesting?
7. Name another improvement in the appearance of the street.

One step further

Imagine you live in Dallas Street.
You have saved £3,000 to improve your house. The house is damp and it has old lead pipes. Lead is a metal which gets into drinking water and is dangerous, particularly to children.

a) Talk with your friends to decide which improvements you think are most needed. Put the improvements in order of importance.

b) Make a list of improvements you can afford with £3,000.

c) Why is it vital to get rid of lead pipes?

LIST OF IMPROVEMENTS	COST (includes materials and cost of labour)
	£
a) Central heating	2,000
b) Electric fires in two rooms	300
c) New kitchen units	1,000
d) New toilet and bath	700
e) Damp course to stop walls getting damp	1,000
f) Replace lead pipes with plastic	200
g) Repairs to leaking roof	800

C   D

FROM VACANT TO OCCUPIED IN JUST 4 MONTHS.

David and Sally's grandmother is staying at their house until the flat she hopes to buy has been improved by Barratts the builders. Look at photos C and D showing these flats in the inner city before and after improvement.

Assignment B

1. How many storeys high are the flats?
2. What building materials are the flats made of?
3. How has the entrance to the flats been improved?
4. Write two sentences describing the flats before and after improvement.
5. Sally and David's grandmother would like to move into a ground floor flat. Why are ground floor flats often the best for old people?

Personal Research A

Find out about part of your town where the urban environment is being renewed or improved. Make a list of any improvements which have been made. Here are some clues to look out for:

a) new roofs, walls, windows and doors,
b) recently planted trees and bushes,
c) sandblasted buildings to remove dirt.

Councils have to make a list of important buildings in their area which should be **preserved**. These are called **listed buildings**. Most of them date from the 18th or 19th centuries. Sometimes whole groups of buildings and spaces are worth preserving because together they look interesting. The council has the power to make the group into a **conservation area**.

E   F    G

Assignment C

Decide which of the buildings in photos E, F, G are worth listing. Give reasons for your answer.

Personal Research B

Find out if any old buildings or unusual objects in your town are listed. Take photographs of some of them.

New Towns

The outer parts of our cities and towns which we call suburbs, have grown rapidly in recent years. Most new houses are built on estates, either council or privately owned. Britain made a bold experiment by building 32 large new communities called **New Towns**. New Towns are special because people who plan them have power to build a whole town not just one estate. They have many trees to make them attractive and grass for leisure. Towns with large green areas are called **Garden Cities**. Some New Towns were built on farmland on what we call **greenfield sites**. Many people think it is wrong to use valuable farmland to build houses when there is derelict land in the inner cities. This is one reason why no more New Towns are being built.

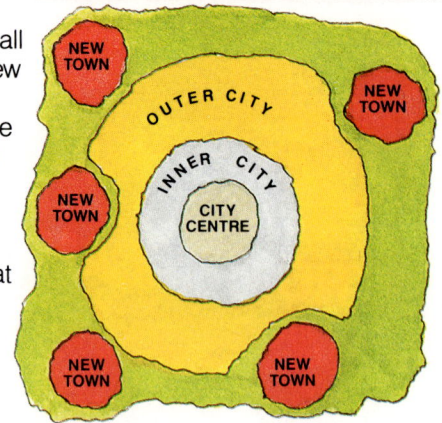

Assignment A

Look at the map of New Towns.

1 Using your atlas make a list of the main cities which are marked.

2 Complete the table:

City	Three nearest New Towns
Bir	
New	
Gl	
Liv	
Bel	

3 Some New Towns have been built on the edge of existing old towns. Two examples are Northampton and Peterborough. What advantages can you think of in building a New Town alongside an existing one?

4 What are the different ways urban renewal and New Towns can help housing problems? Discuss with your friends which is the better solution.

5 How many New Towns are within 100 kilometres of London?

6 How many New Towns have been built in Scotland?

7 Which is the nearest New Town to where you live?

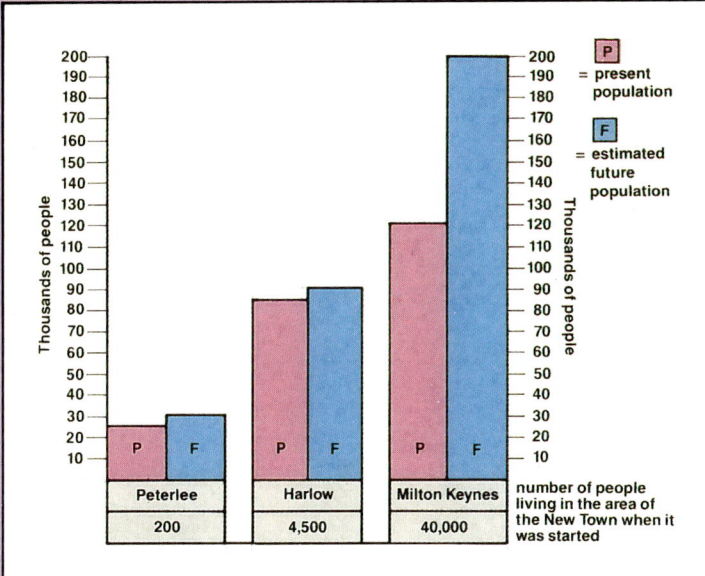

Assignment B

Look at the graph showing population figures for three Towns.

Copy and complete:

'New Towns vary in size from quite small towns like P_____ with a present population of _____ people, to large places like M_____ K_____ with _____ people. Peterlee is planned to grow to only _____, but Milton Keynes will probably grow to become a city of _____ people. H_____ is a medium sized New Town which has nearly reached its planned population of _____ people.'

Not everything about New Towns has been a success. Look at the photographs of houses in various New Towns.

A — Newton Aycliffe
B — Warrington
C — Milton Keynes
D — Runcorn

One step further

1. List the photographs in your order of preference. Give your reasons.

2. What is the difference between the roofs in photographs A and B?

   Why are flat roofs not very suitable for our sort of climate? If part of your school has a flat roof ask your caretaker if there have been any problems with it and what they are.

3. Imagine you were living in one of these places before the building of the New Town began. Write what you think your views would be if you were:
   a) The owner of a village shop.   b) A farmer.

Personal Research

1. Find out the population of your town or district. Is the population growing or getting smaller?

2. Discuss with your friends reasons why the population in your area is changing or not changing.

3. Most areas have a variety of houses, some more popular than others. Make drawings or take photographs of the different houses in your area. Why are some more popular than others?

MILTON KEYNES: LOCATION

Milton Keynes is located between Birmingham and London. It is often called M.K. for short. Look at map A.

Assignment A

1. Which is the fastest route by car to M.K. from
   a) London b) Birmingham c) Heathrow?
2. Which 'A' roads would you use if you travelled to M.K. from a) Peterborough b) Reading c) Birmingham?
3. The green circle on the map has a 50 km radius. M.K. is at the centre.
   How many towns are in the circle?
4. How many airports are within easy reach of M.K.?
5. Half the population of England and Wales can be reached by lorry in three hours from M.K. Why is this important to business people?

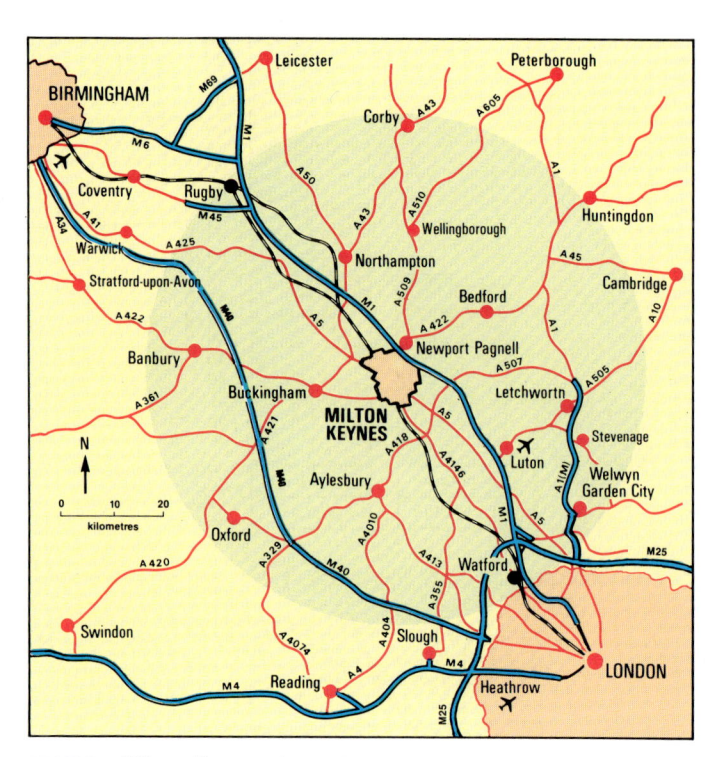

MAP A   Milton Keynes: Location

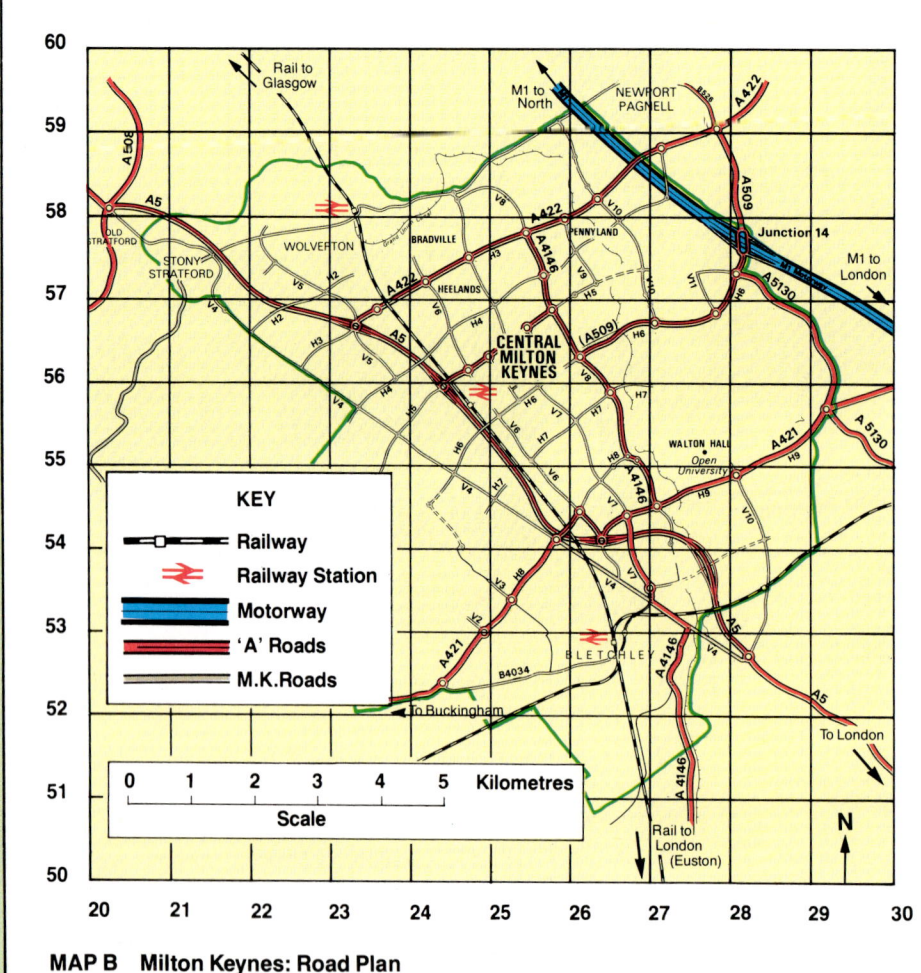

Now look at the road plan of M.K., map B.

Assignment B

1. Travelling from London to M.K., where would you leave the M1?
2. In which grid square is Central Milton Keynes?
3. How many railway stations are shown on the plan?
4. Give their grid references.
5. Where does the railway go from M.K. a) north b) south?
6. Which letter is used for the roads which run
   a) NW/SE b) NE/SW?
   What do you think these two letters stand for?
7. Which roads are unfinished?
8. Draw a plan of what you think the road system will look like when it is completed.

MAP B   Milton Keynes: Road Plan

MAP C Milton Keynes: City Centre

Map A on the opposite page is a small scale map used for finding the best routes to M.K. from outside the area.

Map B is to a larger scale. It is useful for driving around the city but it is not very helpful for finding particular shops or locations.

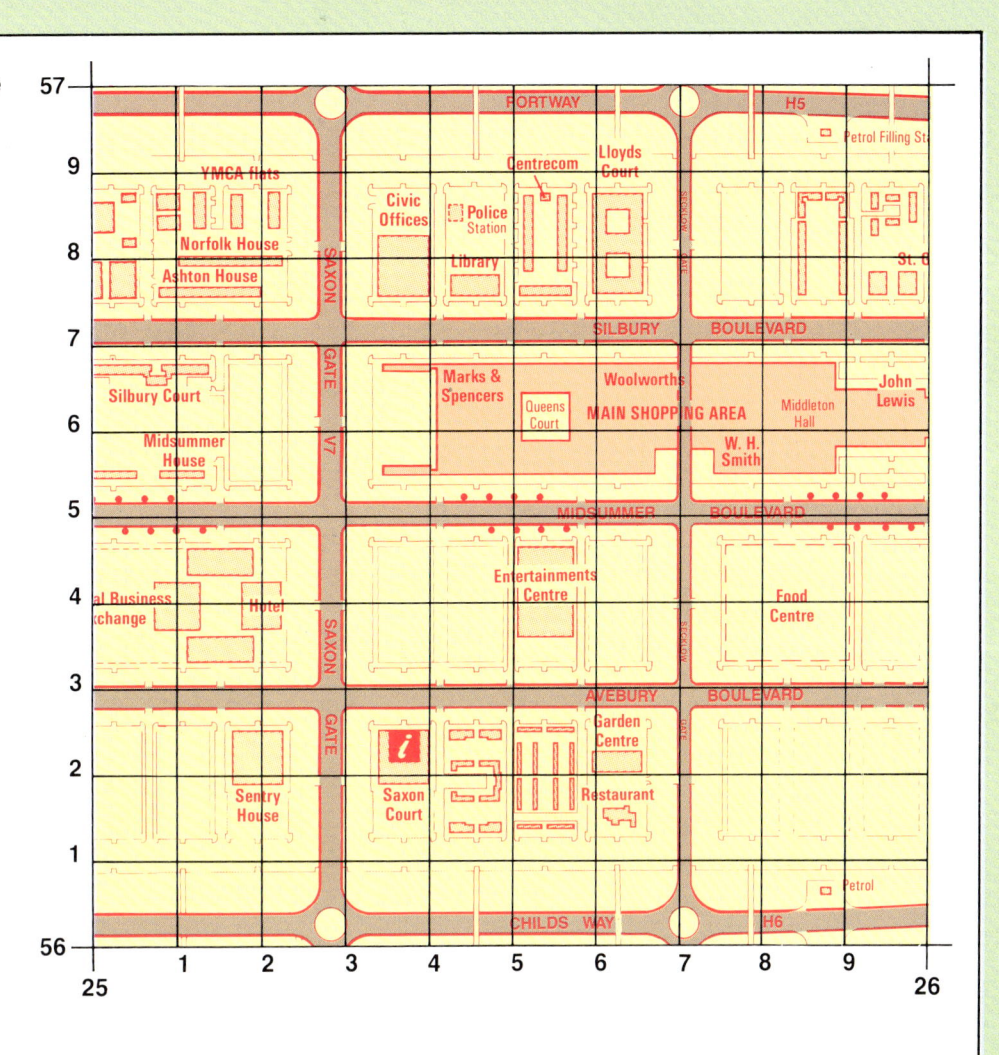

Map C shows **grid square (25,56)** from map B. It is a larger scale map and provides much more detailed information about the city centre.

Grid square (25,56) has been divided into 100 smaller squares. There are 10 squares on the **horizontal axis** and 10 squares on the **vertical axis.**
We can now pinpoint the exact location of a shop or public building by using a **six figure grid reference.**

Follow these instructions carefully.

Place a finger of your right hand on the main grid line 25. Now move east until you reach line 4.
You are now at *easting 254*.

Place a finger of your left hand on the main grid line 56. Now move north until you reach line 8.
You are now at *northing 568*.

Run your first finger up line 254 and your second finger along line 568. The small square where they meet contains the police station. The six figure grid reference for the police station is therefore *(254,568)*.

Assignment C

1. Use the same method to say what is found at the following six figure grid references.
   a) (254,567) b) (259,566) c) (256,566)
   d) (254,566) e) (257,565) f) (256,561)

2. Give six figure grid references for
   a) The petrol filling station.
   b) Tourist information *i*.

One step further

Working with a partner copy and complete the chart.

PERSON	PURPOSE OF JOURNEY	MAP NEEDED
Lorry Driver	Transport goods to Rugby	A
Shopper	To buy house plants	
Holiday maker to the U.S.A.		
		A
		B
		C

MILTON KEYNES: NETWORKS

The map shows two residential areas in M.K. Each area is bounded on four sides by main roads.
When the city was planned it was decided to build a first school in each residential area and a middle school to be shared by two areas.

In M.K. a first school is for children aged 4—8, a middle school is for children aged 8—12.

Assignment A

Which school will be attended by

a) A five year old in Conniburrow?
b) A six year old in Downs Barn?
c) A ten year old in Conniburrow?
d) A ten year old in Downs Barn?

Mr Cook is the deputy headteacher at Conniburrow Middle School. His class have marked their homes on the map opposite. The children who live in the Conniburrow area attended Germander Park First School. Here is a **route network** showing the childrens' homes and their routes to Germander Park First School.

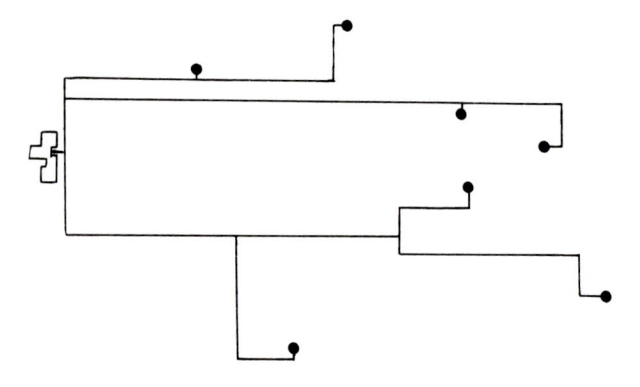

Key:
- • children's homes
- — routes to school

A **network** is a pattern which shows how places are linked.

The link between all the children in this case is the school. The network shows that all the routes meet in one place so we call this a **branching network**.

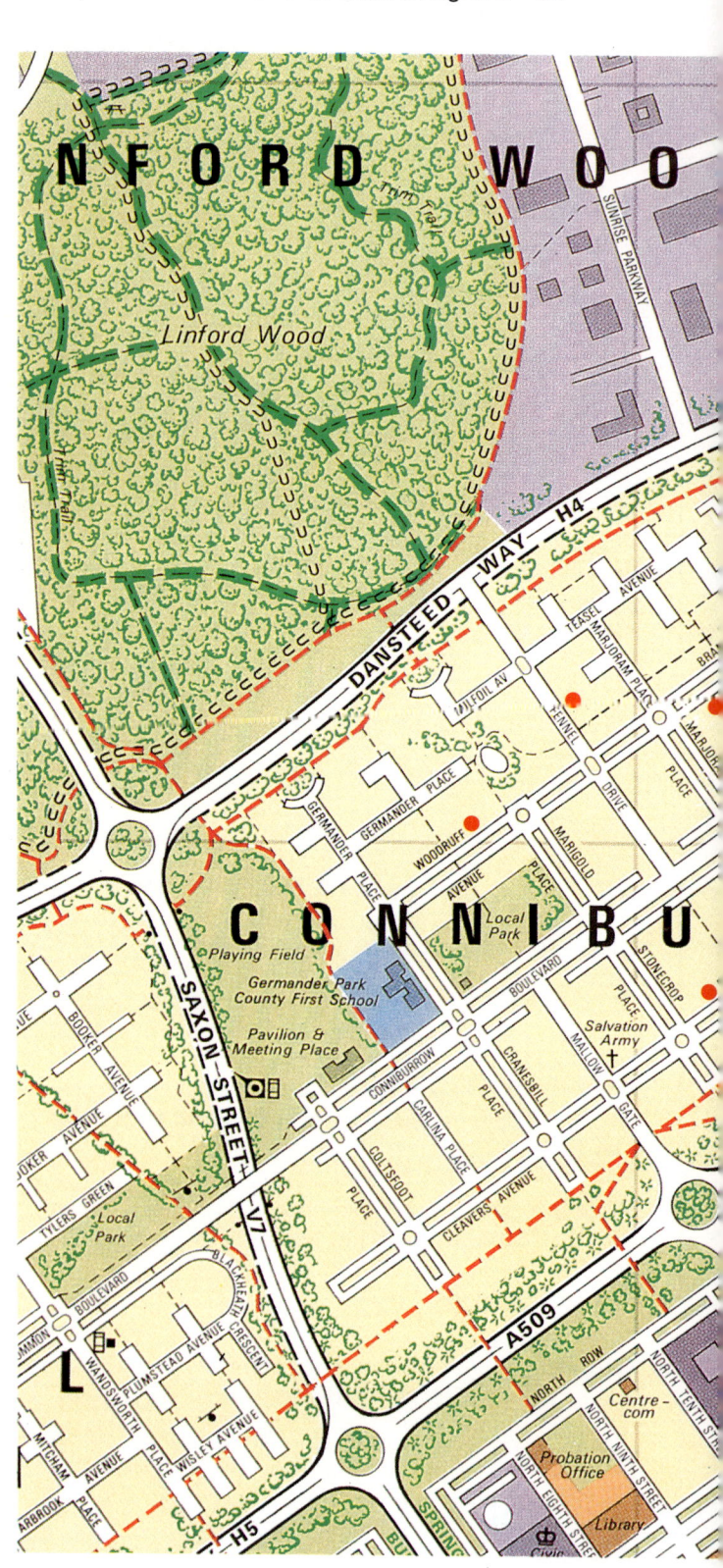

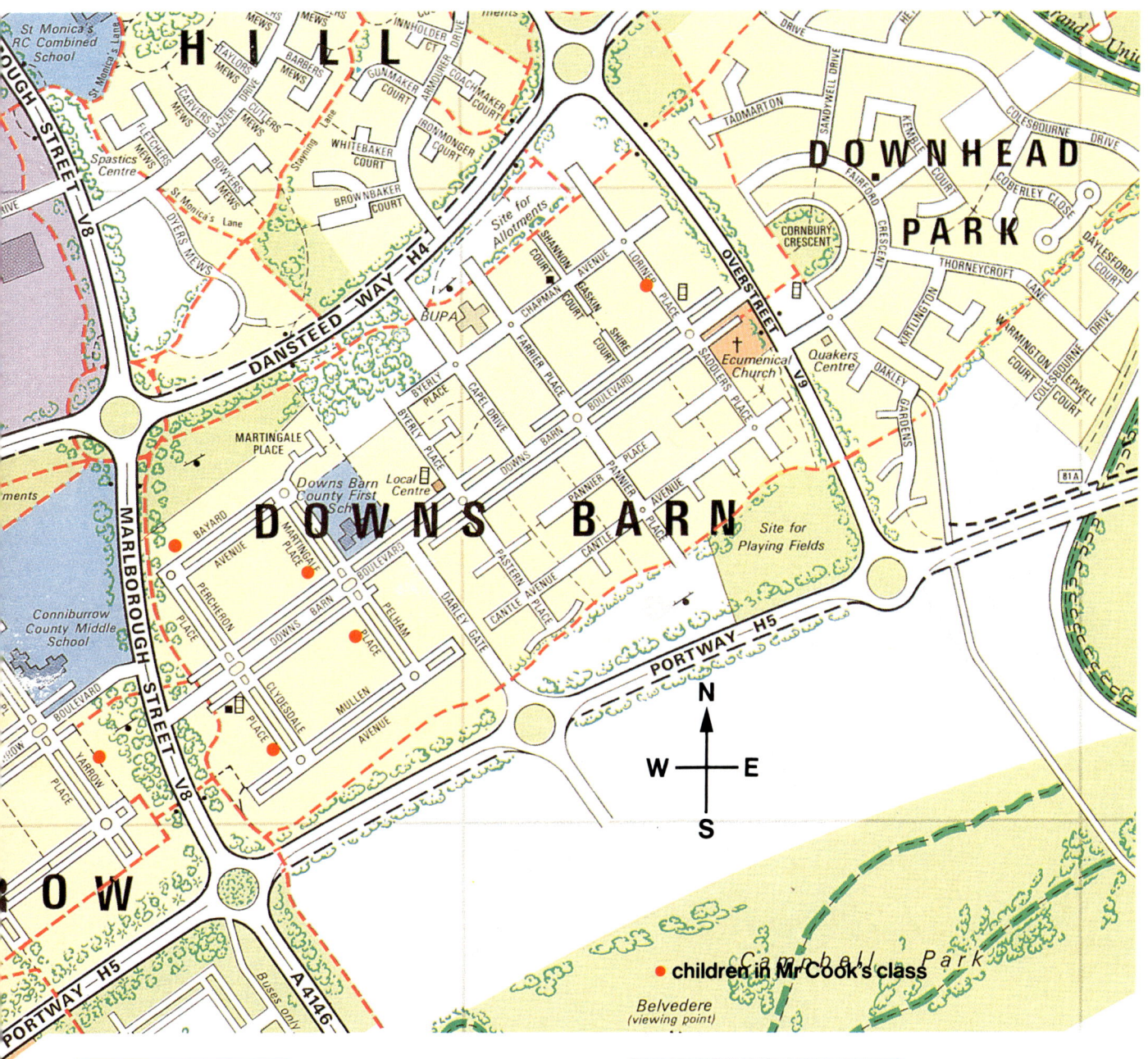

Assignment B

1. Draw the route network for the children living in the Downs Barn area who attended Downs Barn First School.

2. Draw the route network for Mr Cook's class to the middle school. You may find it helpful to use tracing paper.

3. Draw a route network for all the children in the class to the playing fields in the S.E. corner of the Downs Barn area.

One step further

1. Describe the similarities and differences between your area and M.K.

2. Using a map of your school's local area draw a route network for your class.

3. Draw a similar network for the teachers in the school.

4. Compare the two. What differences do you notice?

5. Will a class in your local High School have a similar network to yours? Explain your answer.

GETTING TO DOVER

The map on page 16 shows the motorways and main roads. This chart shows the distances between Dover and some major British cities (in miles).

Dover								
570	Aberdeen							
169	403	Birmingham						
194	503	88	Bristol					
233	513	106	43	Cardiff				
491	145	291	378	393	Glasgow			
275	316	120	209	226	208	Leeds		
73	497	118	117	151	403	195	London	
273	335	87	167	188	215	43	205	Manchester
355	680	273	181	230	561	391	282	351	Penzance

Assignment A

1 Plan routes to Dover from:
   a) Edinburgh b) Newcastle c) Norwich
   d) Plymouth e) Portsmouth f) Anglesey

   Record like this.

PLACE	ROUTE
Carlisle	M6 south to M1
	M1 south-east to M25
	M25 around London to A2
	A2 south-east to Dover

2 How far is it to Dover from:
   a) Aberdeen b) Bristol c) Glasgow d) Penzance?

One step further

1 Use string and the scale bar on the map to work out the distance to Dover from:
   a) Newcastle b) Inverness c) Anglesey d) Ipswich
   If you want your answer to be in km, divide the distance in miles by 5, then multiply the result by 8.

2 Produce a large mileage chart like the one above containing 10 places. Include your nearest town.

3 Use an atlas to find other ports where ferries leave for France.

Assignment B

1 Give the 6 figure grid reference for the following:
   a) Eastern Docks
   b) Lifeboat Station
   c) Dover Castle
   d) Priory Station
   e) Hoverport Terminal
   f) Western Dock Station.

2 Which road runs north-east of the castle?

3 Which road runs west of Priory Station?

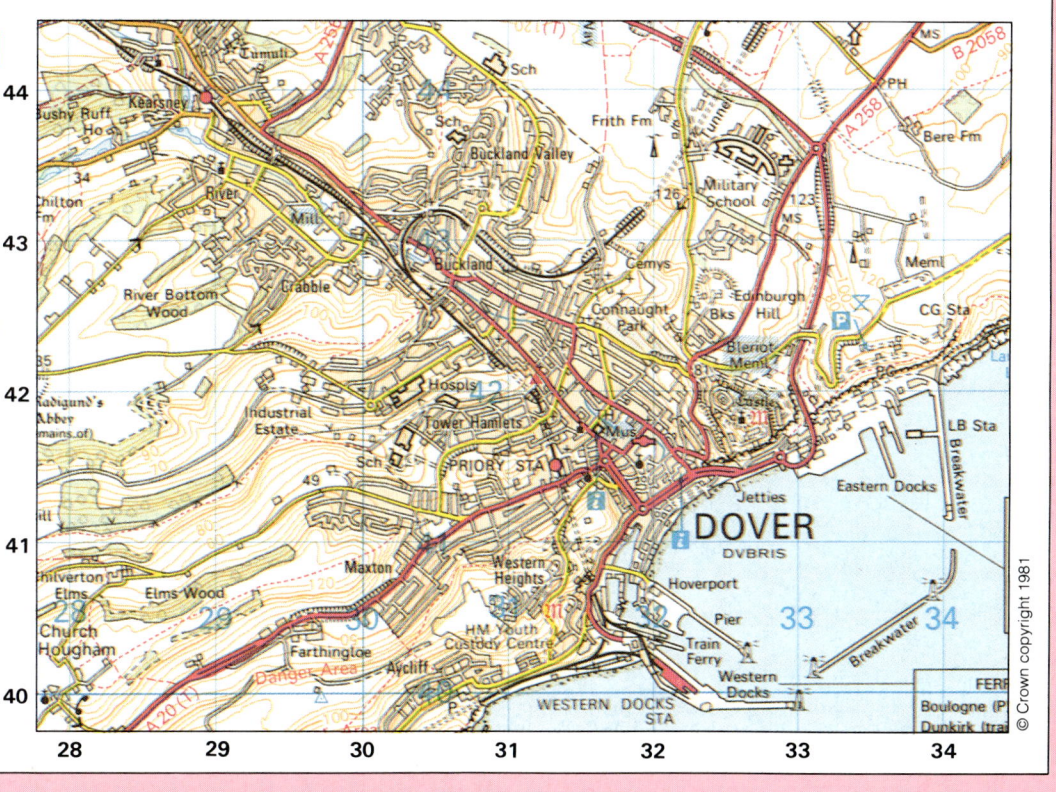

Dover

Assignment

1. How can you tell Dover is an ancient settlement?

2. Look at the photograph and map.

   Copy and complete the chart. Tick which features you can see on the photo or map or both.

FEATURE	PHOTOGRAPH	MAP	BOTH
ferry			
hovercraft			
railway station			
height of tide			
height of land			
Borstal			
road names			

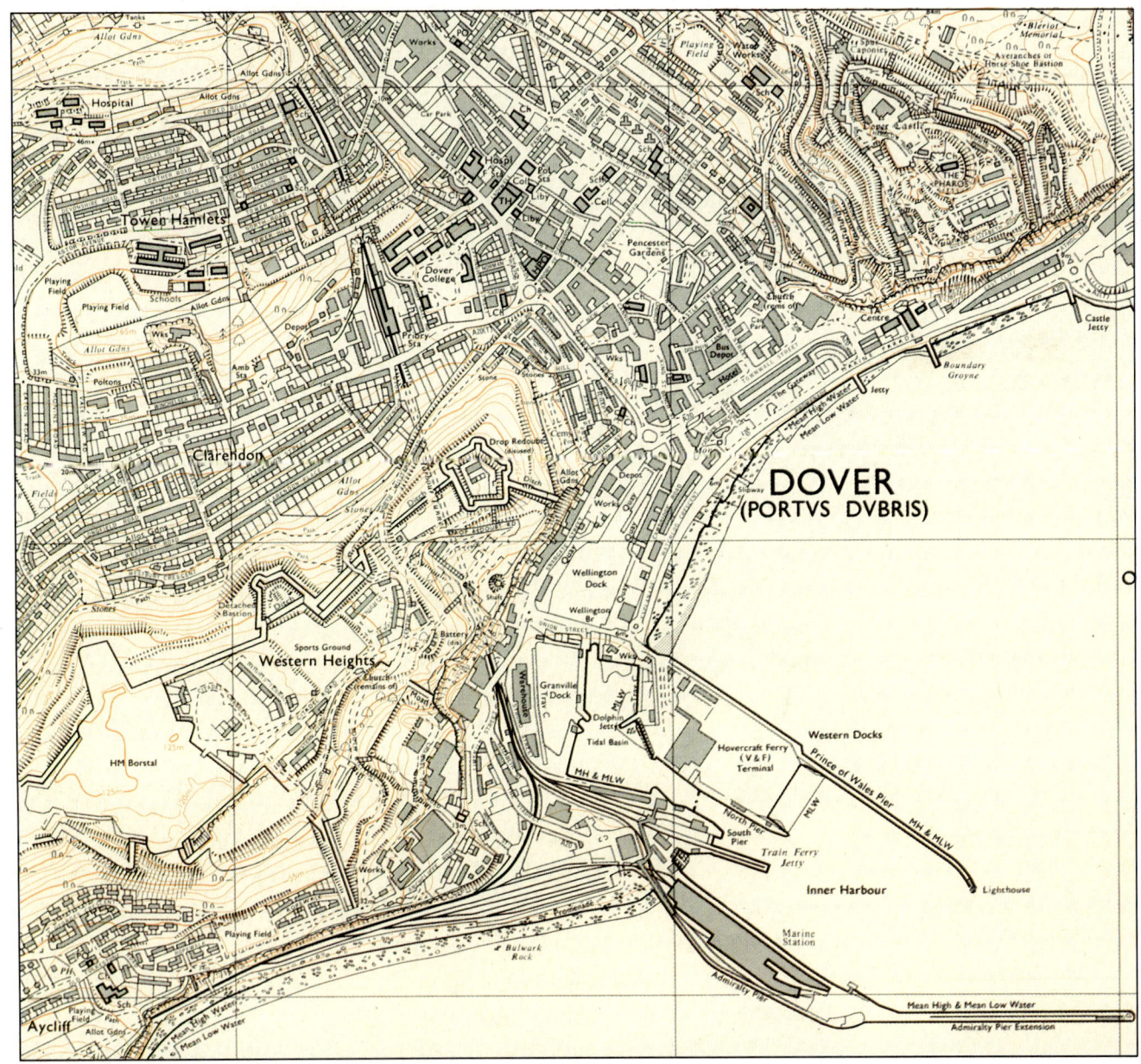

© Crown copyright 1988

One step further

1 Describe and explain the difference between the water inside and outside the harbour.

2 Why is this difference important to ferry and hovercraft companies?

3 Name 3 features the harbour tunnel passes under.

4 Is the map or the photo better for showing:
a) the weather   b) steep slopes   c) vegetation
d) types of industry   e) following a route?

CALAIS

Calais has a long history. For more than 200 years it was ruled by England. Some historic remains date from English rule. It was controlled by the Germans for part of the Second World War.

It has been an industrial town since the middle of the 19th Century. Today the old industries are closing and unemployment has risen.

Assignment A

1. Copy and complete the chart. Give the grid reference for each place and identify the main activity which takes place there.
2. How many of these activities are there in your own locality?
3. Which activities are there because Calais is by the sea?

PLACE	ACTIVITY	GRID REFERENCE
Park		
Campsite		
Beach		
Railway station		
Market		
War Museum		
Hypermarket		
Theatre		
Yacht Basin		
Notre Dame Church		

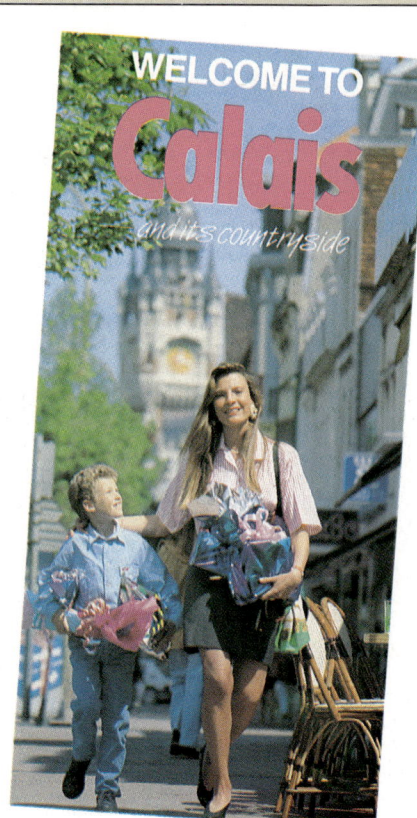

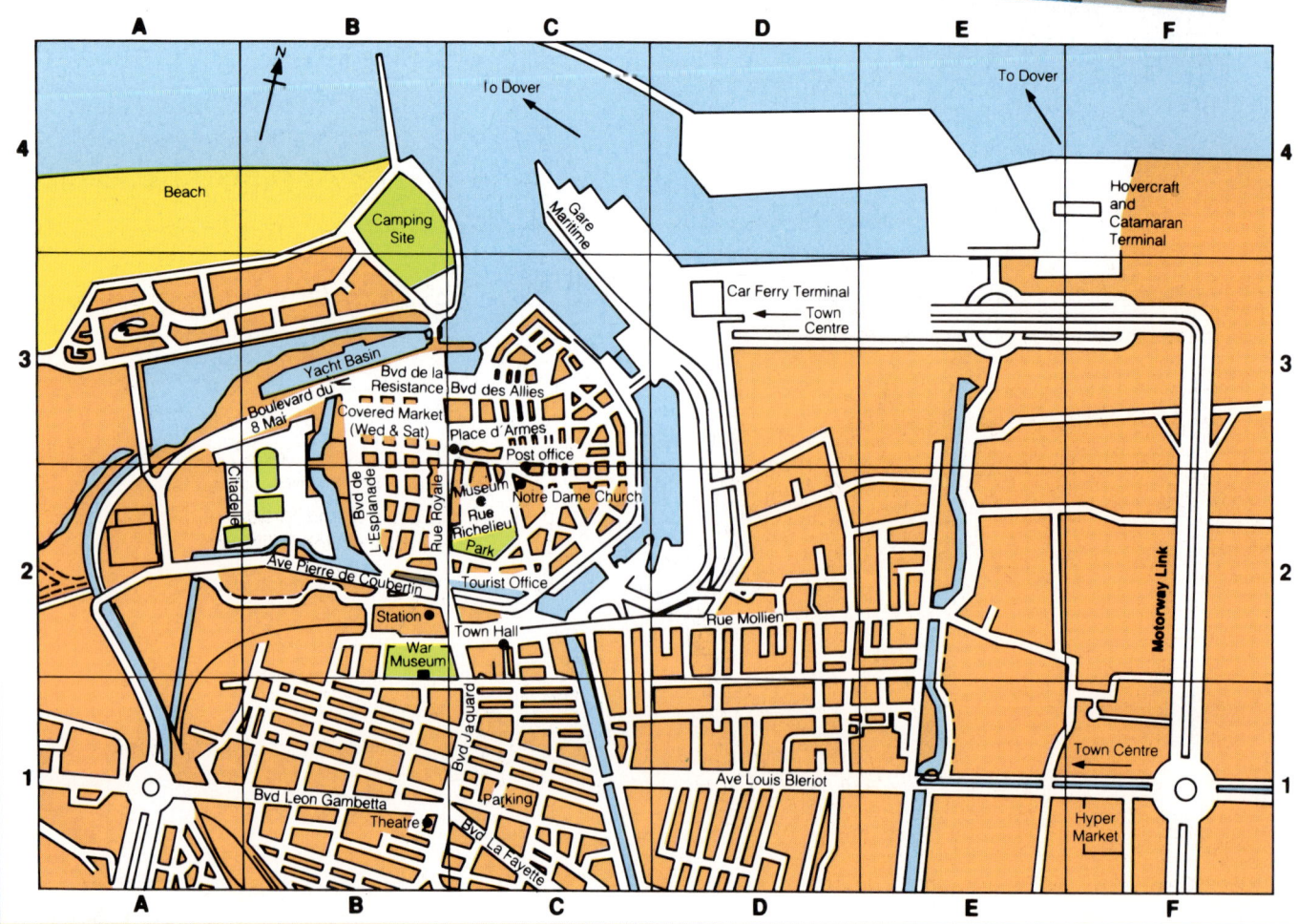

Assignment B

Look at the photo above.

1. What evidence is there that this is not a British street?
2. List the similarities between the street scene in Calais and a street in your nearest town.
3. In which season was this photograph taken?
4. How would the street be different in winter?
5. Give the grid reference for the Church of Notre Dame using the map on page 20.
6. Between which years was it built?
7. Why were Tudor churches not built all over France?
8. List the forms of transport which can use Calais?
9. Why are there two railway stations?
10. How would the following people feel about a motorway link going straight to the docks:

    a) A long distance lorry driver?
    b) A tourist in a hurry to reach Paris?
    c) A shop keeper in the middle of town?
    d) A Calais traffic police officer?

    Explain each answer.

Notre Dame, the only Tudor church in France.

Personal Research

Plan an investigation to find out about the Eurotunnel and how it affects Calais.

CALAIS: A TOURIST TOWN

Most visitors to Calais arrive by ferry and hovercraft. Many pass straight through the town but others stay there for a variety of reasons.

A

B

Shops are for local people as well as tourists.

Assignment A

Look at photo A

1. How do you know this is a tourist locality?
2. How many languages are used on the sign?
3. What is the exchange rate for £1.00?
4. Why do tourists usually need to change money?

Assignment B

1. What could you buy at the shops in photos B and C?
2. What would these shops be called in Britain?
3. Is the shopper in photo D British or French? How do you know?
4. Has he been to a supermarket or a local shop? How do you know?
5. What has he bought?
6. Why do you think someone would travel to Calais to buy this?

C

D

E

F

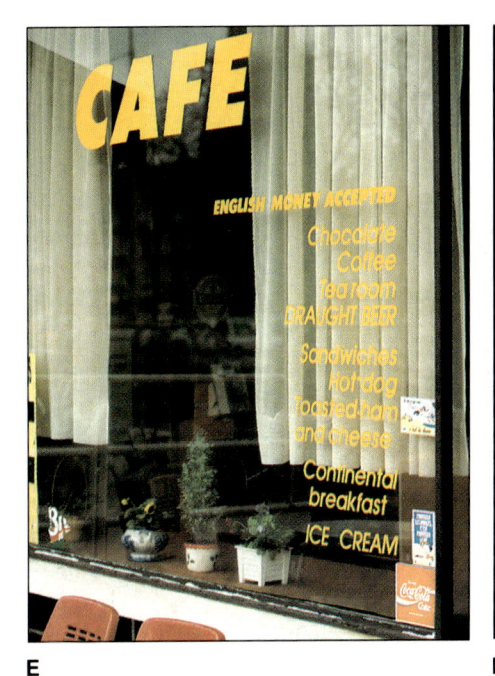

Assignment C

1. How do you know the café in photo E is mainly for British tourists?
2. How is it different from the café in photo F?
3. In how many ways does the 'welcome' poster show stereotypes? Compare it with the 'welcome' picture on page 20. Which is more accurate?
4. What do the following mean:
   a) entrée b) plat garni c) dessert?

One step further

1. Write out the menu from Le Folkestone Brasserie. Give the prices in £ and p.
2. Make a list of the occupations which are supported by tourism in Calais.
3. List the advantages and disadvantages of living in a tourist town. Record like this:

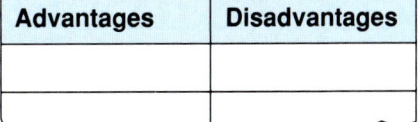

Advantages	Disadvantages

Personal Research

1. Use an English/French dictionary to translate the food on the Coca Cola and Le Folkestone Brasserie menus.
2. Which words on these menus are the same in English and French?

LATITUDE AND LONGITUDE

Sajid asked the teacher whether we can find places on a world map by using a six figure grid reference. Mr Ellis explained that we use a different but similar method.

Sajid was given a piece of paper on which a circle was drawn to represent the earth. He drew a line around the middle of the circle exactly half way between the top **north pole** and bottom **south pole**.

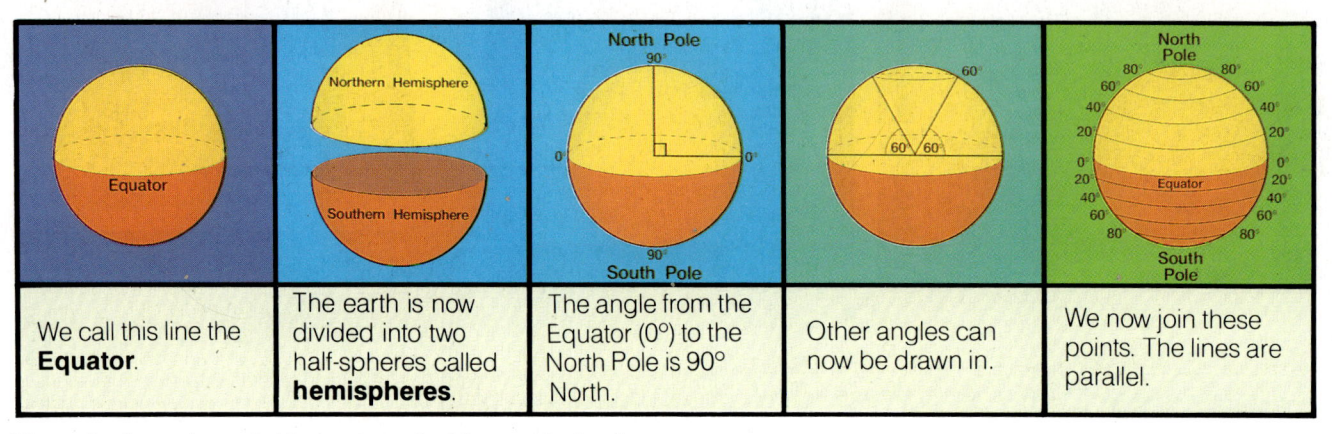

We call this line the **Equator**.	The earth is now divided into two half-spheres called **hemispheres**.	The angle from the Equator (0°) to the North Pole is 90° North.	Other angles can now be drawn in.	We now join these points. The lines are parallel.

These horizontal parallel lines are called lines of **latitude**.

This map shows the outline of the world's countries. Lines of latitude have been drawn on the map for 0°, 20°, 40°, 60° and 80°. You will now need to refer to an atlas.

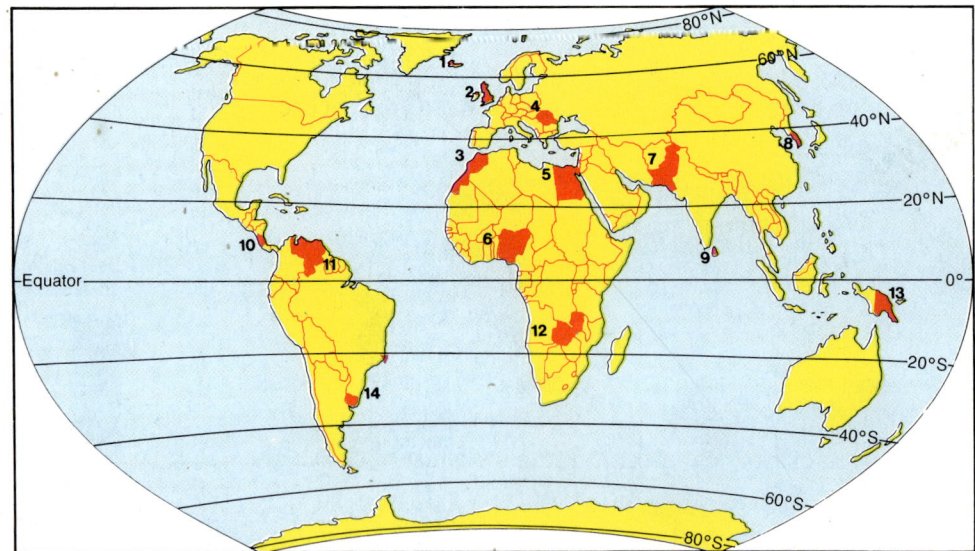

Assignment A

Fourteen countries have been marked on the map.

Identify each one. Do it like this: '1 = Iceland ...'

Now look at the location of the fourteen countries. Remember countries north of the Equator are in northern latitudes, those south of the Equator are in southern latitudes.

a) List the countries in the northern hemisphere.

b) List those in the southern hemisphere.

c) Iceland lies between latitude 60°N and 80°N.

Between which two lines of latitude do each of the other countries lie? Answer like this: 'Papua New Guinea lies between latitude 0° and 20°S.'

Sajid understood that lines of latitude divide the earth into horizontal sections.

He then took other blank spheres and began the process of dividing them vertically.

Any line drawn from the north pole to the south pole is a line of **longitude**. There is no special reason why any particular line should be the starting point 0°, but in 1884 the countries of the world decided that the 0° line of longitude would pass through Greenwich (London).

We call this line the **Prime Meridian**.

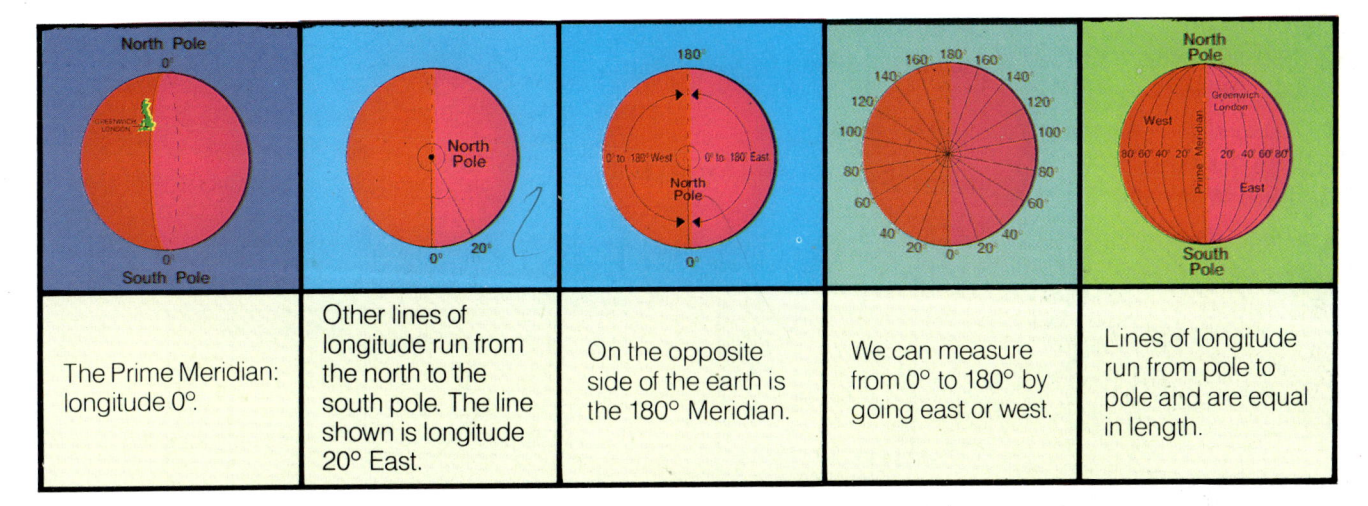

The Prime Meridian: longitude 0°.	Other lines of longitude run from the north to the south pole. The line shown is longitude 20° East.	On the opposite side of the earth is the 180° Meridian.	We can measure from 0° to 180° by going east or west.	Lines of longitude run from pole to pole and are equal in length.

Lines of longitude have been drawn on the map for 0° to 180° West and 0° to 180° East.

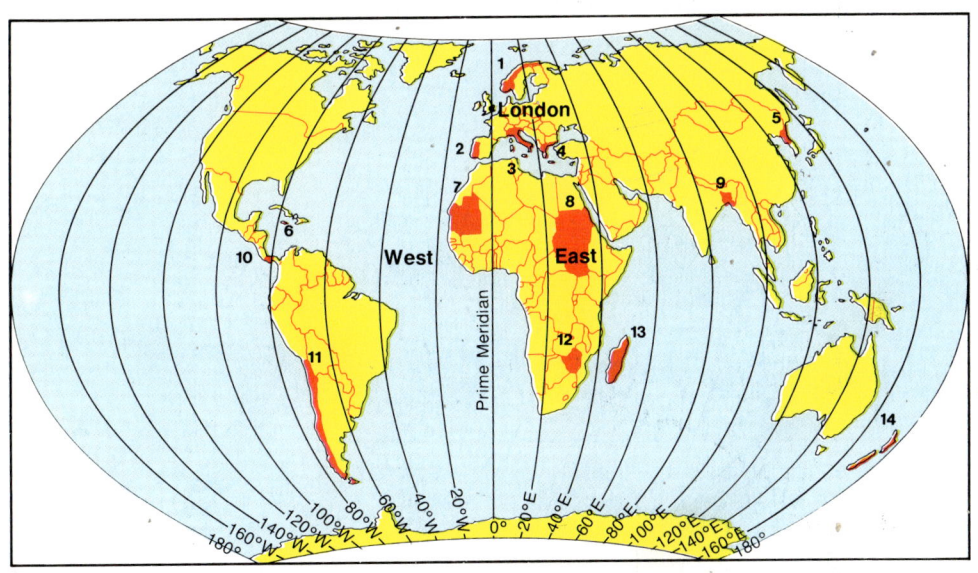

Assignment B

1. Fourteen countries have been marked on the map. Identify each one.
2. List the countries which are west of the Prime Meridian (0°).
3. List the countries east of the Prime Meridian (0°).
4. Between which two lines of longitude does each of the fourteen countries lie? Answer like this:

    'Italy lies between longitude 0° and 20° East.'

One step further

1. On the longitude map list the fourteen countries in sequence. The nearest to 0° should be first, the farthest from 0° last. Remember 20°W of the Prime Meridian is as near as 20°E!
2. Repeat this exercise for the latitude map on the opposite page. The nearest to the Equator should be first, the furthest from the Equator last.
3. Write what you know about the climates of the fourteen countries on the latitude map. Is there a pattern to the distance a country lies from latitude 0° and its climate?

Latitude and Longitude

The world map on the opposite page is a *political* map with lines of latitude (horizontal) and longitude (vertical) drawn on it.

Assignment A

1. Name all the countries through which the following lines of latitude pass:
   a) 40°N   b) 20°S   c) 60°N

2. Name the countries through which the Equator passes.

3. Name all the countries through which the following lines of longitude pass:
   a) 60°W   b) 140°E   c) 20°E

4. Name the countries through which the Prime Meridian passes.

5. By combining information on latitude and longitude we can provide accurate instructions for locating countries.

   Put one finger on latitude 20°N and the other on longitude 80°E. These two lines meet at (20°N 80°E), a point in India.

   We always give references with *latitude* first. We must always remember to put E or W, and N or S, to give a precise reference.

   Name the countries in which the following points are located:
   a) (20°N, 100°W)   b) (30°N, 20°E)
   c) (30°S, 20°E)   d) (30°N, 110°E)

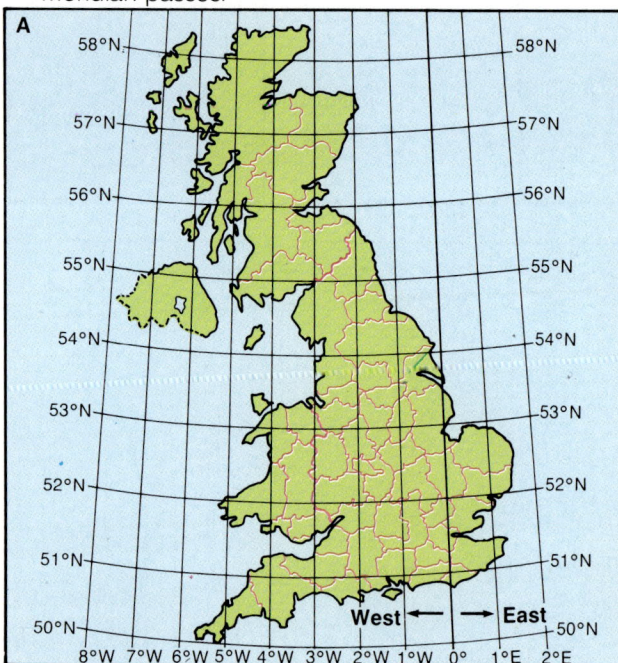

These references are useful but are not always detailed enough. Many places we may wish to locate are not directly on the 10° lines we have been using.

The British Isles lies between latitudes 50°N and 61°N and between longitudes 10°W and 2°E. This map shows the lines of latitude and longitude which cross the British Isles.

We can now give references for locations within Britain. You will need an atlas which shows county boundaries.

Assignment B

In which counties are the following points:

a) (51°N, 1°W)   b) (53°N, 0°)   c) (53°N, 4°W)
d) (54°N, 1°W)   e) (55°N, 7°W)   f) (58°N, 4°W)

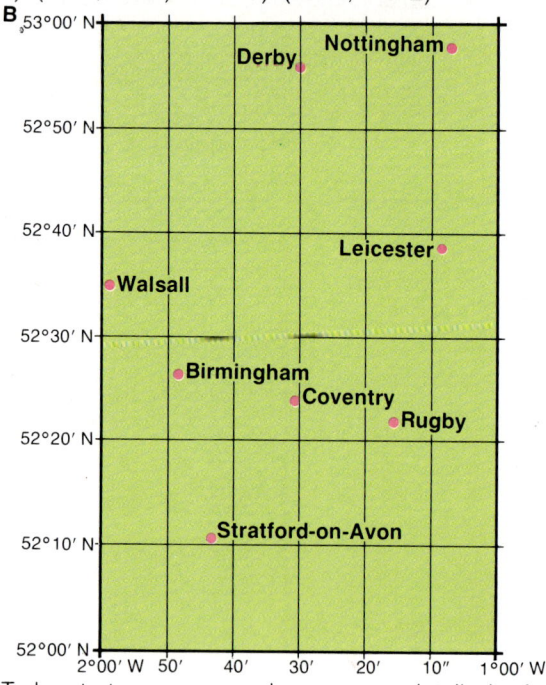

To locate towns we need even more detailed references. We have to divide up each degree into 60 equal parts which we call **minutes**. The sign for minutes is ′.

The reference for London is 51° 30′N (51 degrees 30 minutes North) and 0° 5′W (0 degrees 5 minutes West).

Assignment C

Look at the map of the Midlands. It is the area between latitude 52°N and 53°N and between longitude 1°W and 2°W. The sides of the map have been divided into 10′ (10 minute) sections.

Which four towns are at these points.

a) (52°56′N, 1°30′W)   b) (52°11′N, 1°43′W)
c) (52°35′N, 1°59′W)   d) (52°38′N, 1°8′W)

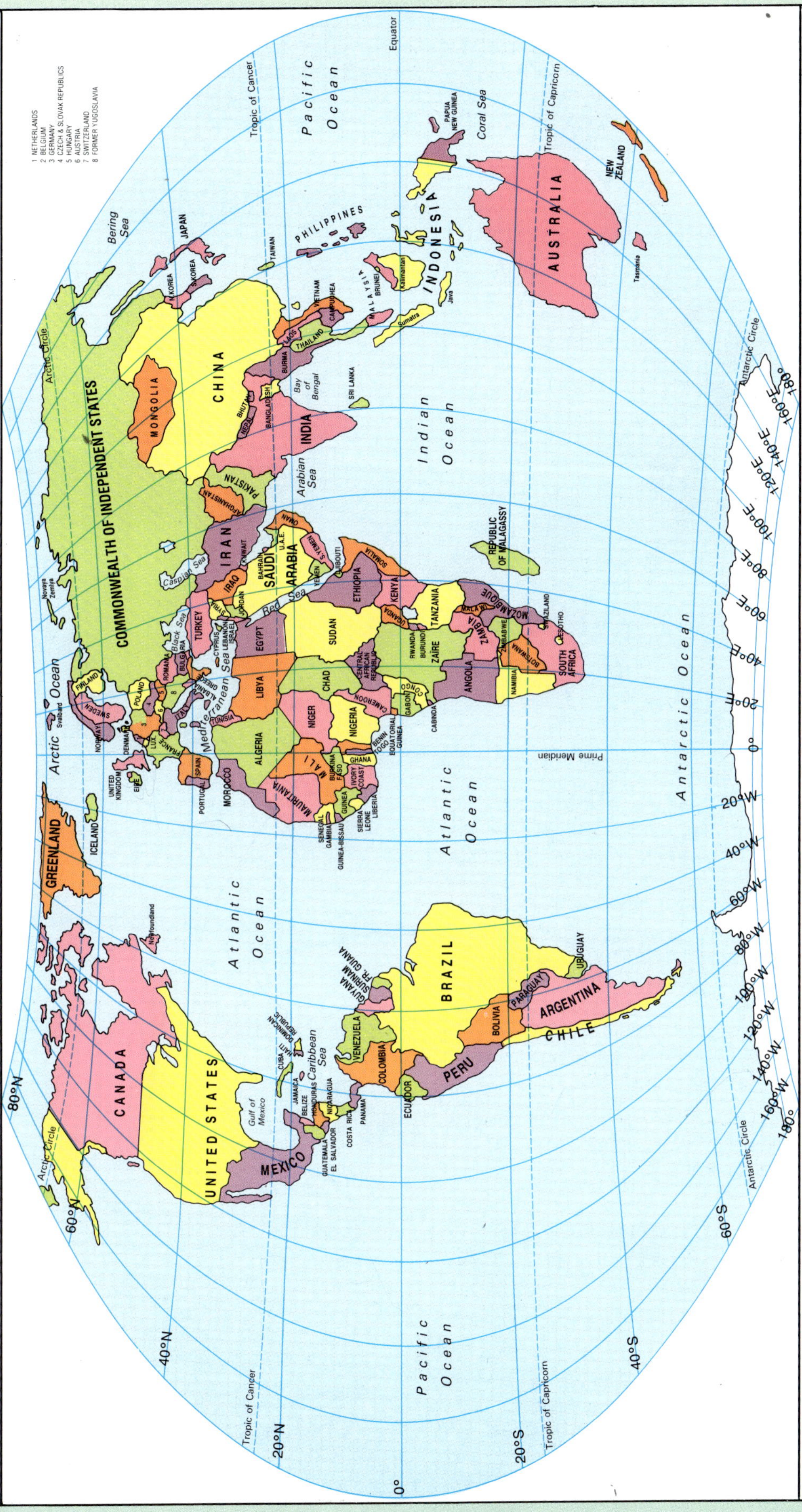
1 NETHERLANDS
2 BELGIUM
3 GERMANY
4 CZECH & SLOVAK REPUBLICS
5 HUNGARY
6 AUSTRIA
7 SWITZERLAND
8 FORMER YUGOSLAVIA
Pacific Ocean
Atlantic Ocean
Indian Ocean
Arctic Ocean
Antarctic Ocean
Bering Sea
Coral Sea
Arabian Sea
Bay of Bengal
Caspian Sea
Black Sea
Red Sea
Mediterranean Sea
Caribbean Sea
Gulf of Mexico
Equator
Tropic of Cancer
Tropic of Capricorn
Arctic Circle
Antarctic Circle
Prime Meridian
COMMONWEALTH OF INDEPENDENT STATES
CHINA
MONGOLIA
INDIA
JAPAN
N.KOREA
S.KOREA
TAIWAN
PHILIPPINES
INDONESIA
MALAYSIA
BRUNEI
Kalimantan
Sumatra
Java
PAPUA NEW GUINEA
AUSTRALIA
NEW ZEALAND
Tasmania
VIETNAM
KAMPUCHEA
THAILAND
LAOS
BURMA
BANGLADESH
BHUTAN
NEPAL
SRI LANKA
PAKISTAN
AFGHANISTAN
IRAN
IRAQ
KUWAIT
BAHRAIN
U.A.E.
OMAN
SAUDI ARABIA
S.YEMEN
YEMEN
JORDAN
SYRIA
LEBANON
ISRAEL
CYPRUS
TURKEY
EGYPT
SUDAN
ETHIOPIA
DJIBOUTI
SOMALIA
KENYA
UGANDA
TANZANIA
RWANDA
BURUNDI
ZAIRE
ZAMBIA
MALAWI
MOZAMBIQUE
ZIMBABWE
BOTSWANA
NAMIBIA
SOUTH AFRICA
LESOTHO
SWAZILAND
ANGOLA
REPUBLIC OF MALAGASSY
CENTRAL AFRICAN REPUBLIC
CHAD
LIBYA
TUNISIA
ALGERIA
MOROCCO
NIGER
NIGERIA
CAMEROON
GABON
CONGO
CABINDA
EQUATORIAL GUINEA
BENIN
TOGO
GHANA
IVORY COAST
BURKINA FASO
MALI
MAURITANIA
SENEGAL
GAMBIA
GUINEA-BISSAU
GUINEA
SIERRA LEONE
LIBERIA
PORTUGAL
SPAIN
FRANCE
LUX
UNITED KINGDOM
EIRE
DENMARK
NORWAY
SWEDEN
FINLAND
POLAND
ROMANIA
BULGARIA
GREECE
ALBANIA
ITALY
ICELAND
GREENLAND
Svalbard
Novaya Zemlya
CANADA
Newfoundland
UNITED STATES
MEXICO
GUATEMALA
EL SALVADOR
BELIZE
HONDURAS
NICARAGUA
COSTA RICA
PANAMA
CUBA
JAMAICA
HAITI
DOMINICAN REPUBLIC
VENEZUELA
GUYANA
SURINAM
FR. GUIANA
COLOMBIA
ECUADOR
PERU
BRAZIL
BOLIVIA
PARAGUAY
URUGUAY
ARGENTINA
CHILE
80°N
60°N
40°N
20°N
0°
20°S
40°S
60°S
180°
160°W
140°W
120°W
100°W
80°W
60°W
40°W
20°W
20°E
40°E
60°E
80°E
100°E
120°E
140°E
160°E

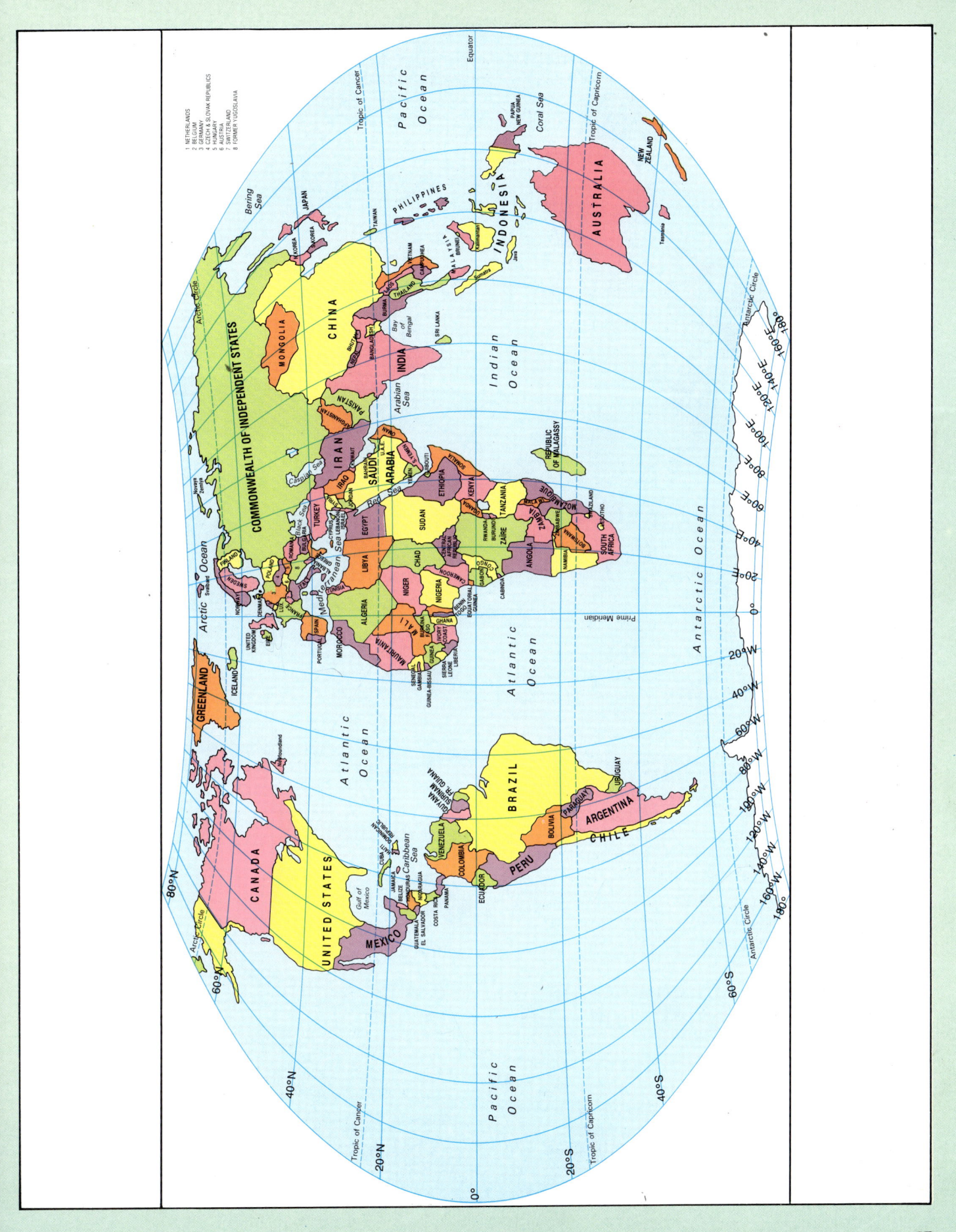

TIME ZONES

Sajid and Sally's class are performing an experiment to help them understand how day and night occur. The four children describe what they can see. Each has a field of vision of 150°. Mr Ellis set up two screens (one light, the other dark) to represent day and night. The children move slowly keeping their heads and eyes looking straight ahead. The direction they move is shown by arrows.

Here are the four statements made by the children. Match the statement to the child.

'I can see only darkness.'
'It's partly light but getting darker.'
'I can see only light, no dark.'
'It's quite dark but getting lighter.'

Mr Ellis explained that the earth revolves just like the four children. When it is light on one side it is dark on the other. When Britain faces the sun we call it daytime. At the same time New Zealand is facing away from the sun so there it is night. We can work out what time it is in other parts of the world by a simple calculation.

The earth is a sphere which we measure as 360°. It takes 24 hours to revolve once. $\frac{360}{24}=15°$, so there is a time difference of 1 hour every 15 degrees. The map opposite is divided into 15° sections, each section represents 1 hour and shows times around the world. It is called a **time zone** map. Large countries are divided into a number of time zones. Some countries choose different zones for convenience. The map shows where this happens.

Assignment A

1. When it is 12 noon in Britain what time is it in:
   a) Portugal b) France c) Cuba d) Chile
   e) New Zealand f) Japan g) India h) Angola?

2. What might children be doing in these 8 countries when it is midday in Britain?

3. When it is 6 p.m. in Britain what time is it in the 8 countries in question 1? (Remember east of Greenwich is ahead of U.K. time, west of Greenwich is behind U.K. time.)

4. a) Which large countries are divided into different time zones?
   b) How many zones does each have?

5. When it is 12 noon in Britain what time is it at the following lines of longitude:
   a) 90°W b) 45°E c) 105°E d) 150°W?

One step further

You will need an atlas showing the world's major cities.

1. Copy and complete the chart.
2. Name the countries.

Tokyo	0600				
Peking		2300			
Delhi					
Dacca					
Cairo			1800		
Lagos					
Paris					
Lima				0900	
Ottawa					
Ankara					
Kabul					1100

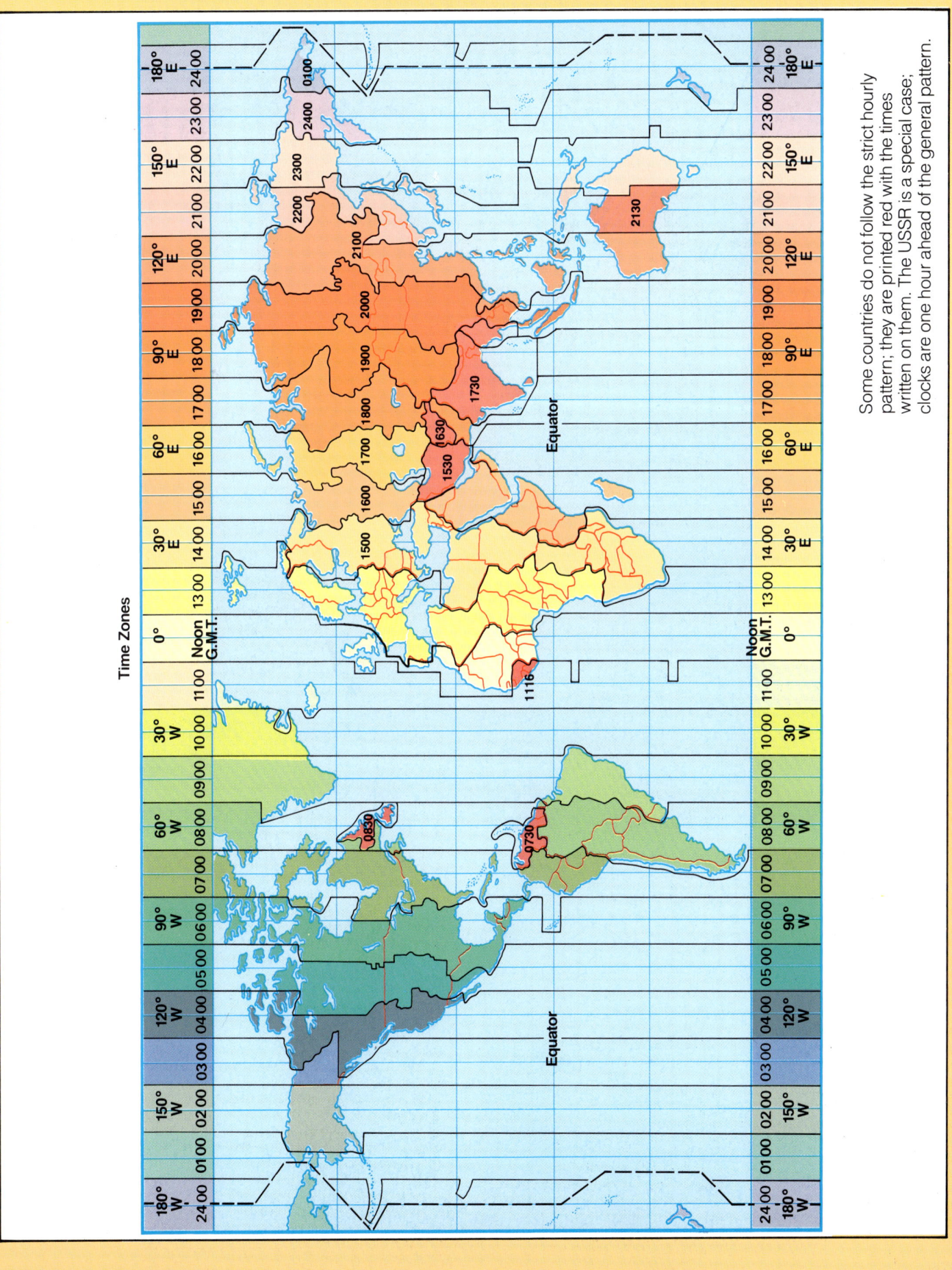

Time Zones

Some countries do not follow the strict hourly pattern; they are printed red with the times written on them. The USSR is a special case; clocks are one hour ahead of the general pattern.

INDIA: URBAN AND RURAL

We can divide the population of the world into two groups. Those who live in towns and cities and those who live in villages and the countryside. People who live in towns and cities are called **urban** dwellers, the rest are known as **rural** dwellers.

These pictograms show the percentages of people who were either urban dwellers or rural dwellers in India in 1901 and 1981.

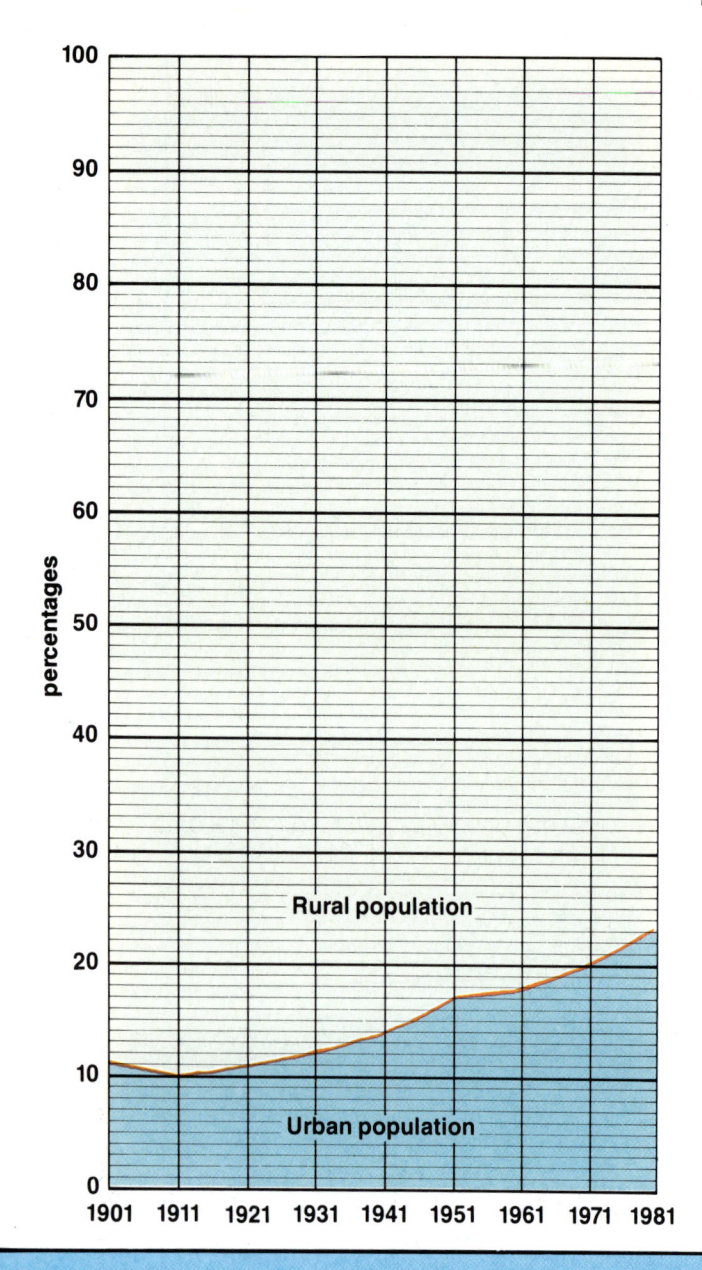

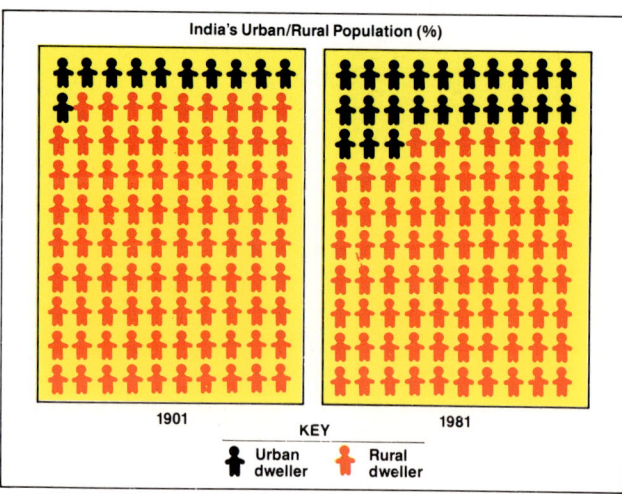

India's Urban/Rural Population (%)

KEY: Urban dweller / Rural dweller

Assignment A

1. Look at the pictogram above.

   a) What percentage of the population lived in towns in 1901?

   b) What percentage lived in towns in 1981?

   c) What is the increase between 1901 and 1981?

2. Copy and complete the chart below by using the information in the graph opposite.

YEAR	URBAN	RURAL
1901	11%	89%
1911		
1921		
1931		
1941		
1951		
1961		
1971		
1981		

   Population in %

   a) In what decade did the percentage of the urban population fall?

   b) In what decade was there the biggest rise?

   c) How large was the change between 1951 and 1961?

   d) How large was the change between 1931 and 1941?

3. Draw pictograms for 1911, 1951 and 1971.

One step further A

1. What percentage of the population were rural dwellers in a) 1921 b) 1961 c) 1971?

2. Copy out the sentence below choosing the correct word:

    'Between 1901 and 1981 the percentage of people living in towns and cities $\frac{\text{increased.}}{\text{decreased.}}$'

3. Which period shows the greatest increase: 1901 to 1941, or 1941 to 1981?

4. Predict the percentage of the population which will live in urban areas by the year 2001.

We can see from the chart and graph that the percentage of the Indian population living in towns has grown throughout the 20th century.

In 1901 only 1 Indian in 10 (10%) lived in urban areas. Today 1 Indian in 4 (25%) lives in an urban area.

When the total population of Britain's towns increased the total population of the rural areas actually fell. Look at the population chart below to discover whether the same is true for India.

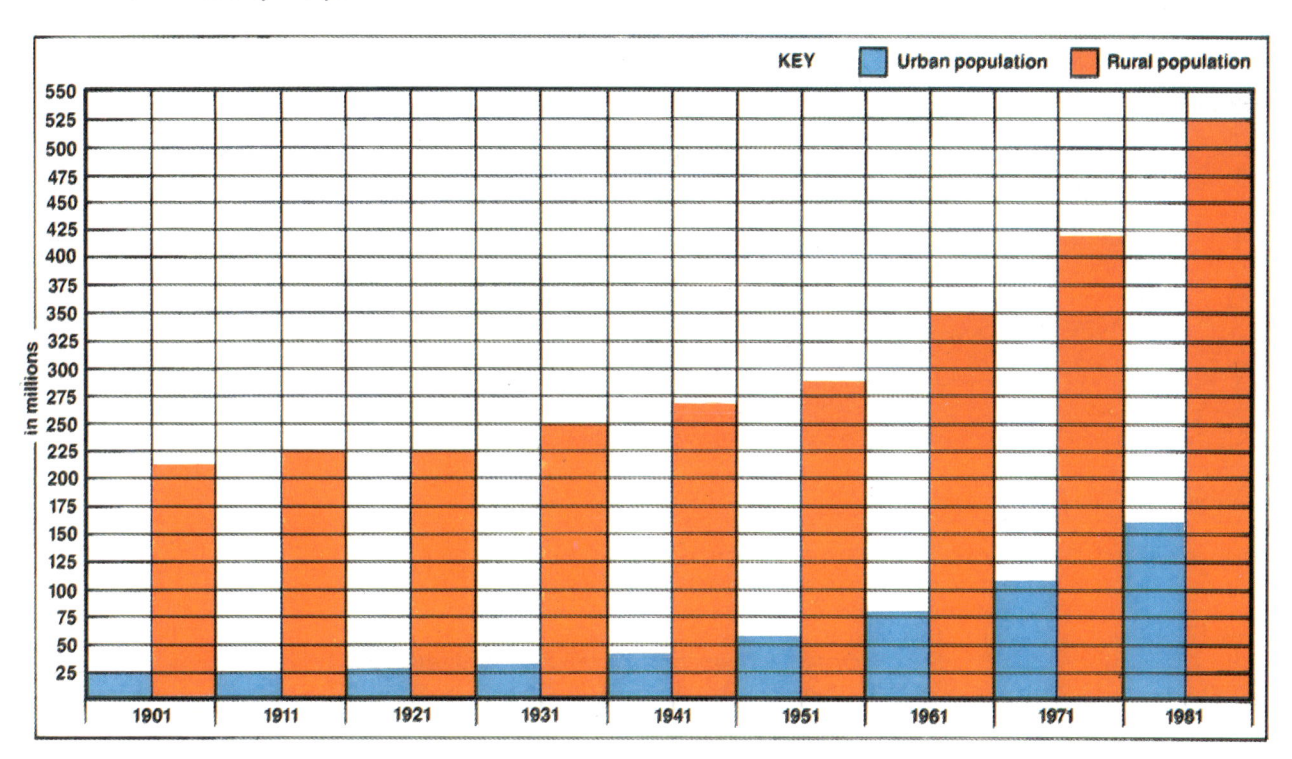

Assignment B

1. Copy and complete the population chart. The population for 1901 has been done for you.

YEAR	URBAN	RURAL	TOTAL
1901	25 millions	212 millions	237 millions
1911			
1921			
1931			
1941			
1951			
1961			
1971			
1981			

One step further B

1. How many more people lived in rural areas than in urban areas in   a) 1901   b) 1951   c) 1981?

2. Copy out the sentences below and choose the correct words:

    'The rural population of India $\frac{\text{rose}}{\text{fell}}$ between 1901 and 1981.'

    'The urban population of India $\frac{\text{rose}}{\text{fell}}$ between 1901 and 1981.'

3. Draw line graphs similar to the one on the opposite page to show
    a) The actual population of urban India 1901-1981
    b) The actual population of rural India 1901-1981.

India: Families and Change

We now know that over the last 40 years the population of India has increased in both urban and rural areas.

One of the main reasons for the increase is the improvement of medical care.

Diseases which once killed can now be controlled. Some diseases have completely disappeared from India. The population rise in rural areas is chiefly a result of better health care. This has also had an effect in the urban areas.

There is a second reason why the urban population has increased. People have moved to the cities in large numbers.

In this section we will look at two families, the Patels and the Sudras, and how changes have affected them.

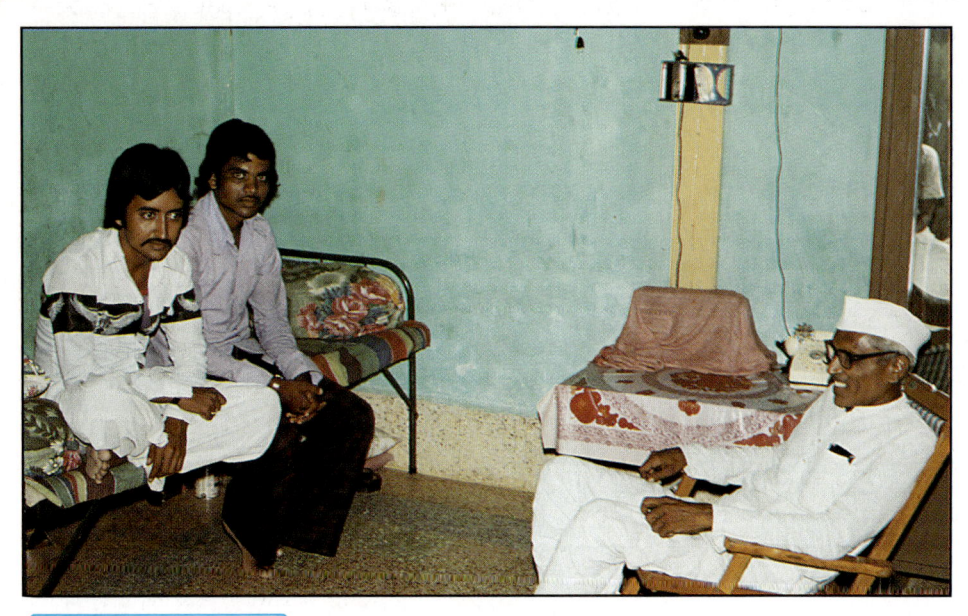

The Patels are a family who own 25 hectares of good farming land. They have lived in the village for generations. They are one of the richest families. Living in the home are Mr and Mrs Patel and their two sons and two daughters.

Assignment A

The house above belongs to the Patels, the one below is the Sudra's home. Write a description of the two homes. Think about: size, building materials, electricity supply and general appearance.

The Sudras are a poor family. They own only 1½ hectares of land. The land they own is not as good as the Patel land. The Sudra family has lived in the village for generations. As well as farming their fields Mr Sudra works on the Patel farm for wages at harvest time. The Sudras have six children, four girls and two boys.

"I need a loan so I can buy seeds, fertiliser and machinery."

There have been many changes since the 1950's which have affected farmers.

- New roads have been built all over India making communications between rural and urban areas easier: farmers can now sell their produce to the city markets
- Electricity is available in many rural areas
- Improved water supplies are available
- Better types of seed can be bought, producing a much larger harvest
- Artificial fertilisers are available which can greatly increase production
- Machinery can be bought to speed up work on the land

Mr Patel and Mr Sudra both went to a government official to arrange to borrow money.

"Certainly you can have the money you have asked for at 10% interest."

"I'm sorry. We cannot lend you any money."

Assignment B

In order to borrow money for farming a person needs **security**. This is usually land. If the borrower cannot pay, the lender can seize the land and sell it to repay the loan.

1. Who has the best security Mr Sudra or Mr Patel?
2. Who has been granted the loan?
3. Describe how you would feel if you were Mr Sudra.
4. Mr Sudra still wanted to borrow the money. He went to the village money lender and asked for a loan. Why does the private money-lender charge a higher rate of interest?
5. Do you think it is fair that the richer farmer can borrow money at a cheaper rate?
   Can you think of a way to help Mr Sudra?
6. What would happen to Mr Sudra's farm if he did not borrow the money he wanted?
7. How much interest will Mr Patel pay on a loan of 1,000 rupees?
8. How much interest would Mr Sudra pay on the same size loan?

"This land is poor. It is not good security. I will charge you 20% interest."

Personal Research

1. If you went into the local bank and asked for a personal loan to buy a bicycle what do you think the manager would say? Why?
2. Find out which of the following could probably obtain a bank loan, give your reasons: a tramp, a dentist, a married person without a job, a foreign holidaymaker, a teacher.

INDIA: SUCCESS AND FAILURE

Mr Patel used his loan to buy the following:

Bank of India Loan 10% interest

- Tube well
- Seeds 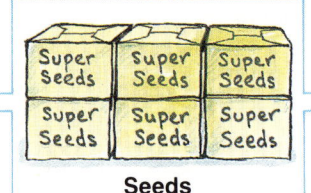
- Tractor 
- Fertiliser and Insecticides 

The farm grew more than ever before. Lorry loads of food were sent to the city for sale.

Produce sent to market

HIGH PROFITS

- Mr Patel's second son is sent to college.
- The Government loan is repaid.
- The eldest son goes to work in Kuwait.

Assignment A

1. Explain how the tube well, seeds, tractor, fertiliser and insecticides helped Mr Patel's profits.
2. If you were Mr Patel and had paid back your loan how would you feel?
3. India's new roads helped Mr Patel. Before the roads were built it took too long to reach the city. Explain how this would have affected Mr Patel's produce.

Mr Sudra used his loan to buy the following:

Money lender loan 20% interest

- Bullock
- Seeds
- Persian Wheel
- Fertiliser and insecticides

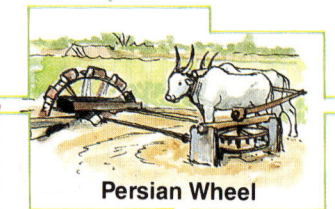

The Sudra's land produced more than before. The Sudras worked on the land. At busy times Mr Sudra earned extra money by working for Mr Patel.

Sells surplus in village

LOW PROFIT

- Mr Sudra's children are sent to the village school.
- The Sudra family are well fed and healthy.
- Mr Sudra repays part of the loan.

Assignment B

1. How did Mr Sudra spend his loan?
2. Why has Mr Sudra not been able to repay the whole loan?
3. Why do the new roads not help Mr Sudra as much as Mr Patel?

One step further A

1. The Sudra children now go to the village school. Before the changes they had to help on the land.
   Describe how Mr and Mrs Sudra felt about their children receiving an education.
2. Why cannot Mr Sudra send one of his children to work in Kuwait?

DROUGHT

For the following two years there were problems for all the farmers. The rain they relied on did not fall.

Money from the eldest son working in Kuwait paid for the electricity.

The son who was educated left to work in the city.

The electric tube well pumped up water from deep below the ground. Mr Patel could water half his land in this way.

▽ **SMALL PROFIT**

The Patel Farm.

Mr Sudra was told there was no work for him.

The drought caused food shortages, prices rose, Mr Patel sent less to market but sold for high prices.

He told his wife he had lost his job.

The bullock had to be sold. There was no money to buy food for it.

The Sudra children were needed to help on the land.
Every effort was made to save the crops from dying.

▽ **NO MONEY**

The Sudra farm.

Insecticides kill crops if there is no rain.

The money lender demanded repayment of the loan or the Sudra land instead. The Sudras were forced to leave their farm. They moved to the city to look for work.

One step further B

1. List the factors which worked in Mr Patel's favour.
2. List the factors which worked against Mr Sudra.
3. Why could Mr Sudra not borrow more money to feed his bullock?
4. How did Mr Patel obtain water?
5. Why could Mr Sudra not obtain it?

One step further C

1. Where did Mr Patel get the money to keep his well pumping?
2. Describe how Mr Patel cut his costs.
3. How could he manage without his son and Mr Sudra?
4. Can you explain why a shortage of a product results in a higher price?
5. Why did Mr Sudra not benefit from higher prices?

A FUTURE IN THE CITY

Dipak Patel moved to the city, bought a house and started a printing business. His qualifications and his father's support made it easy for him to borrow money for a printing press. His business is a success. The family owns a car, a colour T.V., stereo and 'fridge. A cleaner works for them every day and a woman deals with the washing four times a week. The children are educated in English at school. Holidays are spent visiting Grandad or at famous places such as Delhi and the Taj Mahal.

Pradip Sudra moved to the city. The family collected scrap materials and built their own one-roomed shanty. The nearest water supply was 200m away. Pradip went out each day to look for work. He would do anything: building, selling, cleaning, portering, digging ... Some days he was lucky, other days he found nothing. His wife, Amita, sometimes worked on a building site with two of the children. All the family searched for work in order to survive. Unless Pradip could find a regular job they knew that school was not possible for the children.

Assignment A

1. Describe the homes of the Patels and Sudras. Think about location, size, materials, style, facilities.
2. Describe the work both men do. Think about location, regularity, pay, tiredness, variety.

Personal Research A

1. Use a map to locate the following tourist attractions: Delhi, Jaipur, Agra, Bombay, Varanasi (Benares).
   Try to find photographs of each city.
2. Discover what you can about the Taj Mahal and Old and New Delhi. What attractions do they have for tourists?

One step further A

1. How do you think Mrs Patel spends her time?
2. Write a diary describing a day in Mrs Sudra's life.
3. Why might the family be upset if Mrs Sudra becomes pregnant?
4. Why do the Patels think their children will have a better chance of success in life if they can read and speak English?

Dipak's day

KEY			
	Working		Visiting friends
	Sleeping		Reading
	Eating		Temple
	Watching T.V.		Travelling to work
	Shopping		Travelling to wash
	Playing with children		Home repairs
			Searching for work

Pradip's day

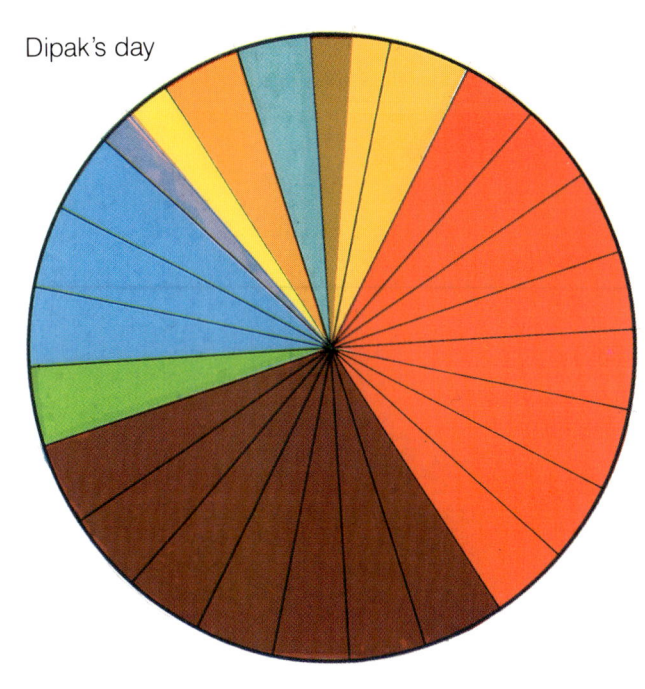

ACTIVITY	DIPAK	PRADIP
Sleeping		
Eating		
Working		
Temple		

Assignment B

1. Copy and complete the chart.
2. What fraction of Pradip's day is spent sleeping?
3. What fraction of Dipak's day is spent working?
4. What appears only in Dipak's chart?
5. What appears only in Pradip's chart?
6. List the similarities and differences in the two charts.
7. Why is there no mention of holidays in the information about the Sudras?

One step further B

1. Write your feelings about life in the city
   (a) From Pradip's point of view.
   (b) From Dipak's point of view.
2. What part of Pradip's day do you feel is wasted? Explain your answer.
3. If Pradip finds a permanent job
   a) How would his pie chart change?
   b) How might his children's day change?

Personal Research B

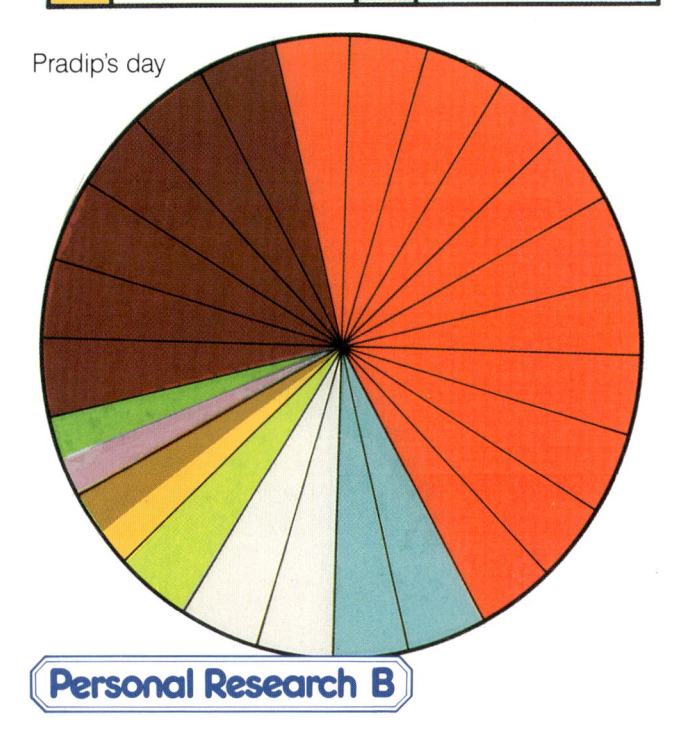

Choose an adult person you know well.

Ask them for information about their typical day.

1. Draw their 24 hour pie chart.
2. Whose chart is theirs closest to in the Patel and Sudra families?
3. List the similarities and differences between the chart you have drawn and one of the Indian charts.
4. Now construct a pie chart for yourself.
5. Compare your day with the days of Pradip's and Dipak's children.
6. Imagine you are either Pradip's child or Dipak's child.
   Write a diary describing your day and draw a pie chart like those on these pages.

UPS AND DOWNS

How can we show ups and downs on a flat map? Map-makers a long time ago drew pictures on their maps to show hills and mountains. Some people say they look like molehills or sugar loaves. Look at part of Christopher Saxton's map of Cheshire dated 1577.

Assignment A

1. How old is this map?
2. The south-west corner of Saxton's map shows a part of Wales called Flint. Does Saxton show the hills of Flint the same size as or bigger than the Wirral hills?
3. Do Saxton's 'molehills' give a good idea about:
   a) How steep the land slopes?
   b) What the real shape of the land is?
   c) How high the hills really are?
   Explain your answers.

This sketch map of a small town called Longridge shows how arrows can be used to mark slopes. The arrows point down the slope telling us which way the ground slopes.

KEY
- ⇚ very steep
- ⇐ fairly steep
- ← gentle slope
- flat
- P playing fields
- housing areas

Assignment B

1. Name two roads which are very steep
2. Is Market Place lower or higher than Derby Road? How can you tell?
3. Which school is built on a fairly steep slope and which on flat ground?
4. Why do old people who live in Derby Road find it hard to walk to the Library?
5. Which will probably be the best playing field to sledge on **P1, P2 or P3**?

One step further

Draw a map to show the roads around your school or home. Put arrows to show the slopes on your map area. Even towns in flat areas have some steep slopes. Think about bridges, river banks and railway embankments.

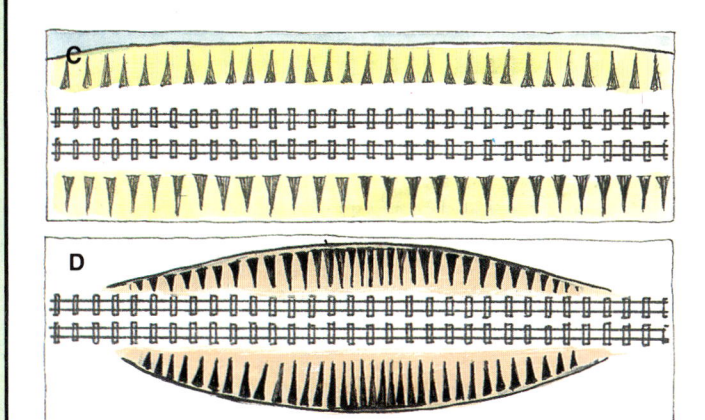

A better idea for showing how the land slopes is to use little wedge shaped lines called **hachure lines**. Hachures are still used on maps today to show steep slopes such as railway embankments and cuttings. The narrow end of the wedge shape points downhill. Steep slopes can be shown in heavy black hachures and gentle slopes in light grey hachures.

Assignment C

Look at maps C and D and match them with pictures 1 and 2.

1. Which map shows the railway in a steep sided cutting?
2. Which map shows the railway on an embankment?
3. Explain how you can tell the difference on the maps.

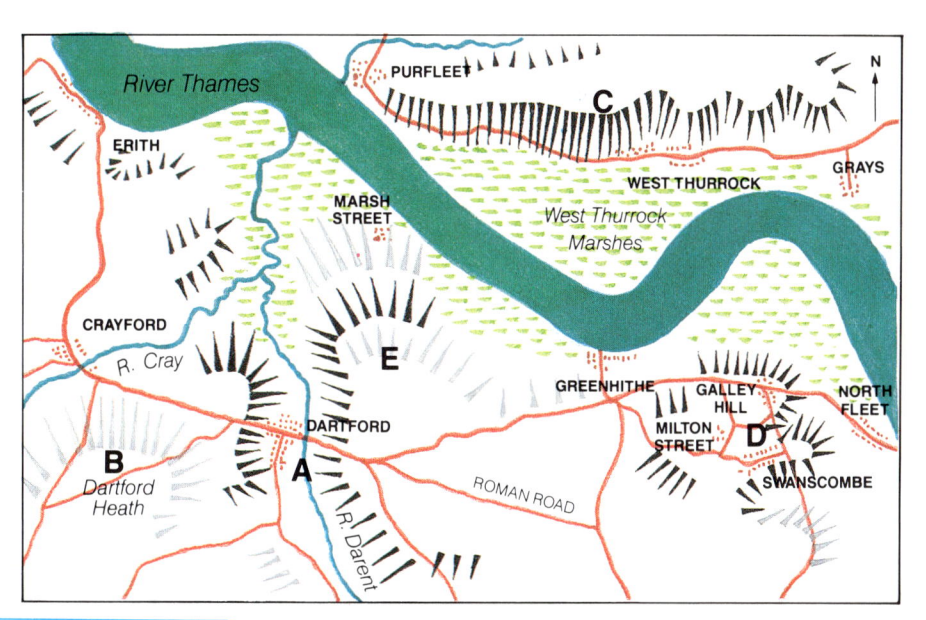

Assignment D

Look at map E based on an 1805 Ordnance Survey map of the Thames Valley near Dartford and West Thurrock.

1. How are slopes shown on the map?
2. Look at the places marked **A**, **B**, **C** and **D** on the map.
   Match the look of the hachure lines at these places with these descriptions:

   a) There are several hills with very steep sides, and villages on the top of the hills.

   b) This is a long ridge of high ground, with a steep slope to the south over marshy ground.

   c) This small town is where a Roman Road crosses a river. There are very steep valley sides on the east and west of the town.

   d) The land here slopes very gradually, for a long way, down from the heath.

3. Describe the slope north of **E** and how it changes down to Marsh Street.

CONTOURS DOWN

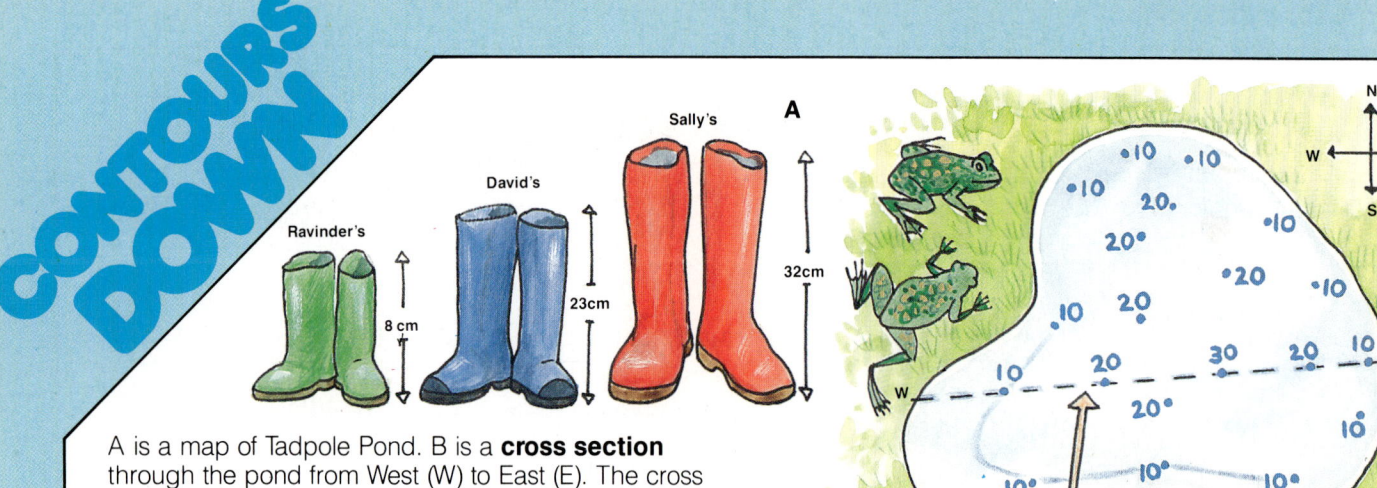

A

A is a map of Tadpole Pond. B is a **cross section** through the pond from West (W) to East (E). The cross section shows three layers of water, shallow, medium and deep.

B

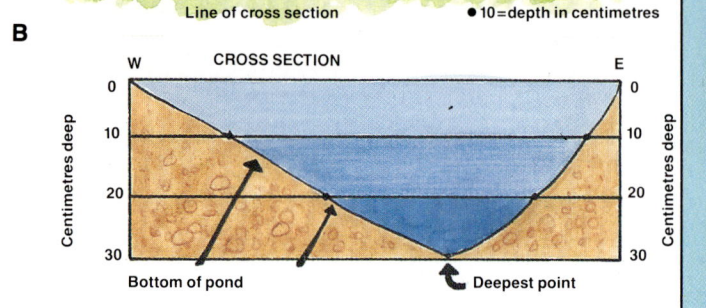

Assignment A

1. Copy or trace the map of Tadpole Pond and put on the depths in centimetres.
2. Complete the line joining the 10 centimetre depth points near the edge of the pond.
3. Draw the 20 centimetre depth line.
4. Shade the area deeper than 20 centimetres dark blue, the area between 10 and 20 centimetres medium blue, and the area shallower than 10 centimetres light blue.
5. How deep is the deepest point in Tadpole Pond?
6. Who would get water in their wellies if Ravinder, David and Sally walked along the cross section line through the pond?
7. Look at the cross section. Which side of the pond has the steepest slope, the west or the east?
8. Why is even a shallow pond like this a danger to young children?

The three areas of dark, medium and light blue on your map of Tadpole Pond show three different layers of water depth. We call this a **layer-coloured map**. The lines joining points of equal depth (or equal height) we call **contour lines**.

One step further A

1. What are the depths of the two contour lines on your map of Tadpole Pond?
2. Draw a large pond with a different shape. Give it a name. Mark in depths of your pond from 1 metre near the shore to 5 metres near the middle. Draw four underwater contour lines showing depths of 1, 2, 3 and 4 metres.
3. Shade the areas between the contour lines to make a layer-coloured map.

Personal Research

Using your atlas or a globe find out the deepest parts of these seas and oceans, and complete the table.

SEA OR OCEAN	DEPTH OF DEEPEST PART	NAME OF DEEP WATER AREA
North Sea		
Mediterranean		
Atlantic		
Indian		
Pacific		

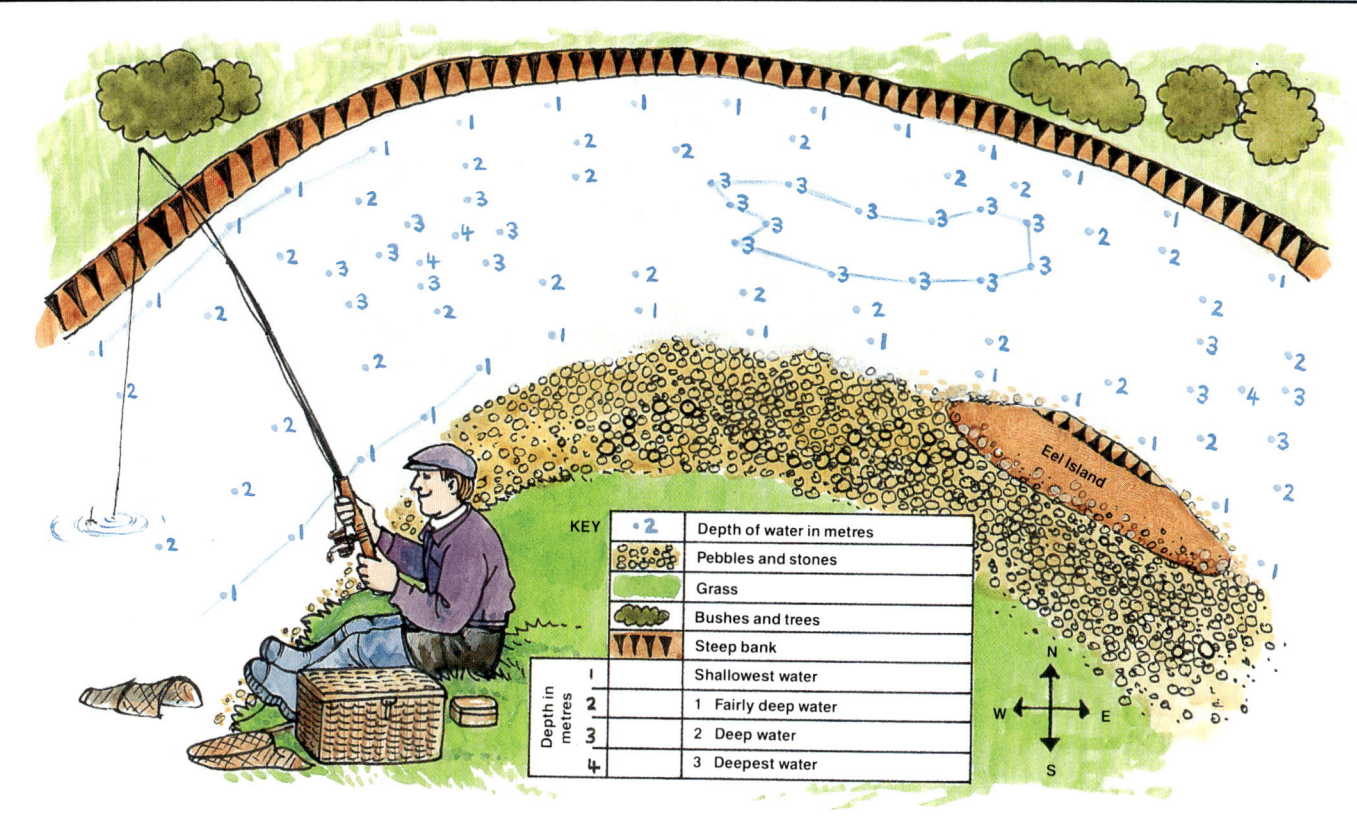

Sally and David's father is a keen fisherman. The biggest fish lie in deep pools in the deepest part of the River Trout. Their father has drawn this map showing depths in various parts of the river. You have to find where the fish are by drawing contours and making a layer-shaded map.

Assignment B

1. Lay tracing paper over the map of the River Trout and draw the banks of the river and Eel Island.

2. Complete the 1 metre underwater contour line along the south bank of the river.

3. Complete the other 1 metre underwater contour, by joining points marked 1 metre deep along the north bank.

4. Now draw the 2 metre underwater contour along the south side, and another 2 metre contour depth along the north side.

5. Join points 3 metres deep to find the deepest 'pools' in the river. One has been done for you.

6. Shade water deeper than 3 metres, dark blue; between 2 metres and 3 metres, medium blue; between 1 metre and 2 metres, light blue. Leave the shallow water (less than 1 metre) white.

7. Fill in the depth key with the correct blue colours.

8. How deep is the deepest point of this part of the River Trout?

9. How many deep 'pools' (deeper than 3 metres) in the river are there?

10. Which side is covered with pebbles and stones?

One step further B

Your map of Trout River shows underwater contours at depths of one metre, two metres and three metres. We say this contour map has a **vertical contour interval** of one metre. If the contours are drawn at 10 metres, 20 metres and 30 metres the vertical contour interval is 10 metres.

1. What is the vertical contour interval on your map of Tadpole Pond?

2. Draw a map of a river with an island in the middle of the river. Mark in depths of water from 1 to 5 metres. Show the water gradually getting deeper from the river banks, and then getting shallower near the island. Draw underwater contours at a one metre interval. Shade the different depths of water to make a layer coloured map. Name the river and the island.

3. Imagine you were marooned on the island. The water is infested with flesh eating fish. Describe how you would escape.

CONTOURS UP

Look at the layer coloured map of the land near the old town of Lewes. Lewes is in the County of East Sussex.

MAP A

CROSS SECTION — Line of section A—K

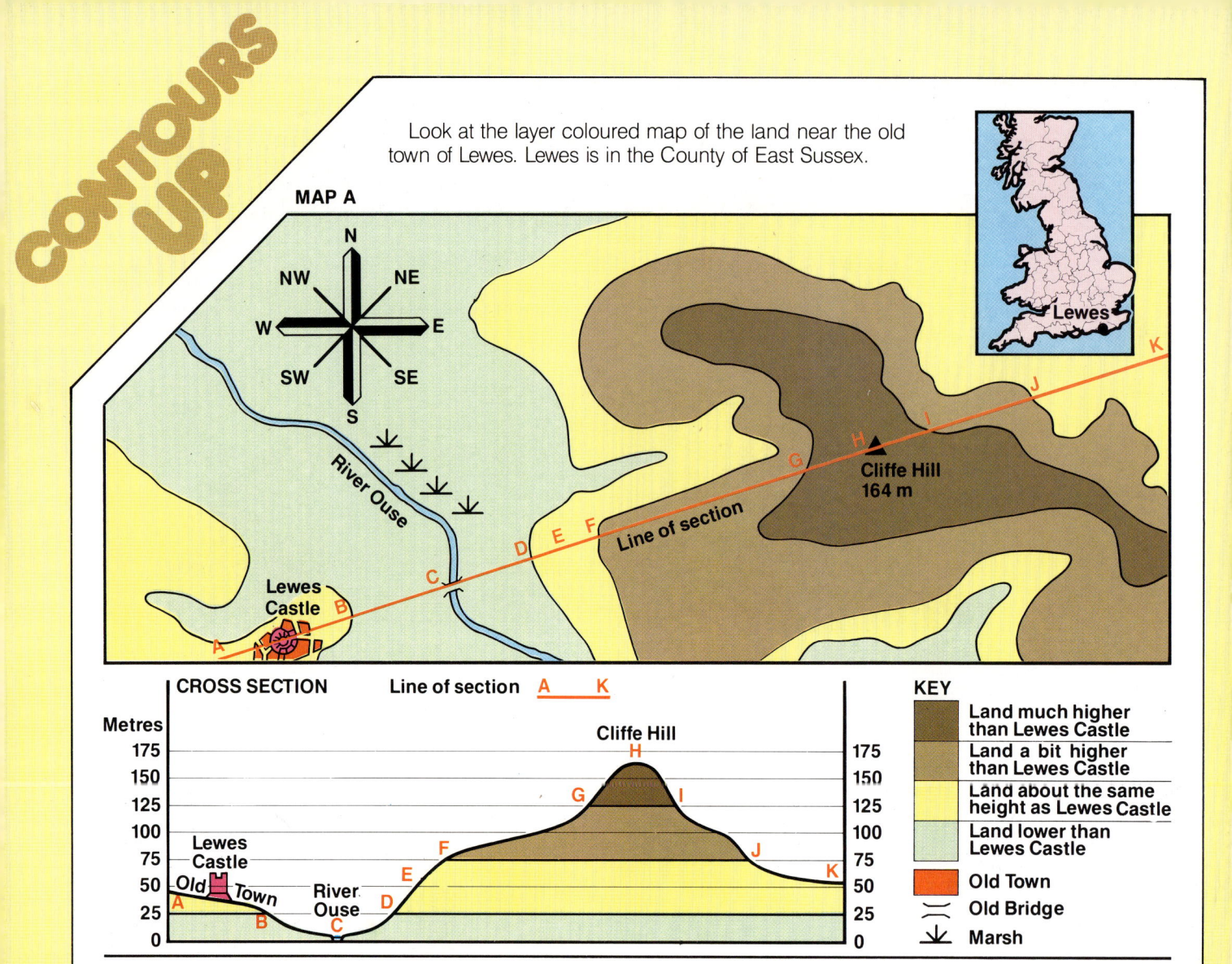

KEY
- Land much higher than Lewes Castle
- Land a bit higher than Lewes Castle
- Land about the same height as Lewes Castle
- Land lower than Lewes Castle
- Old Town
- Old Bridge
- Marsh

Compare the layer coloured map (Map A) with the cross section A–K which cuts through the hill on which Lewes Castle stands and through a bigger hill called Cliffe Hill.

Assignment A

1. On map and section which colour shows land higher than Lewes Castle?
2. Which colour is the land lower than Lewes Castle?
3. How high is Cliffe Hill?
4. In which compass direction are we walking from Lewes Castle to Cliffe Hill?
5. Imagine you are walking from A to K along this section. Complete these sentences correctly:

    'From A to B the land slopes down past Lewes Castle. At C we cross the _____.

    From C to D the land slopes $\frac{down.}{up.}$

    From D to E the slope is very $\frac{gentle.}{steep.}$

    From E to F the slope continues $\frac{up}{down}$ but more gently.

    At F we are just $\frac{lower}{higher}$ than Lewes Castle and standing at _____ metres.

    The land $\frac{falls}{rises}$ steadily through G to H.

    H is at the $\frac{bottom}{top}$ of Cliffe Hill.

    From H to I the land slopes $\frac{up.}{down.}$

    From I to J the route down is $\frac{gentle.}{steep.}$

    We finish at K which is at about $\frac{150}{50}$ metres.'

One step further A

Write down some reasons why this was a good piece of land on which to build the old town of Lewes. Why was Lewes not built on the top of Cliffe Hill?

MAP B

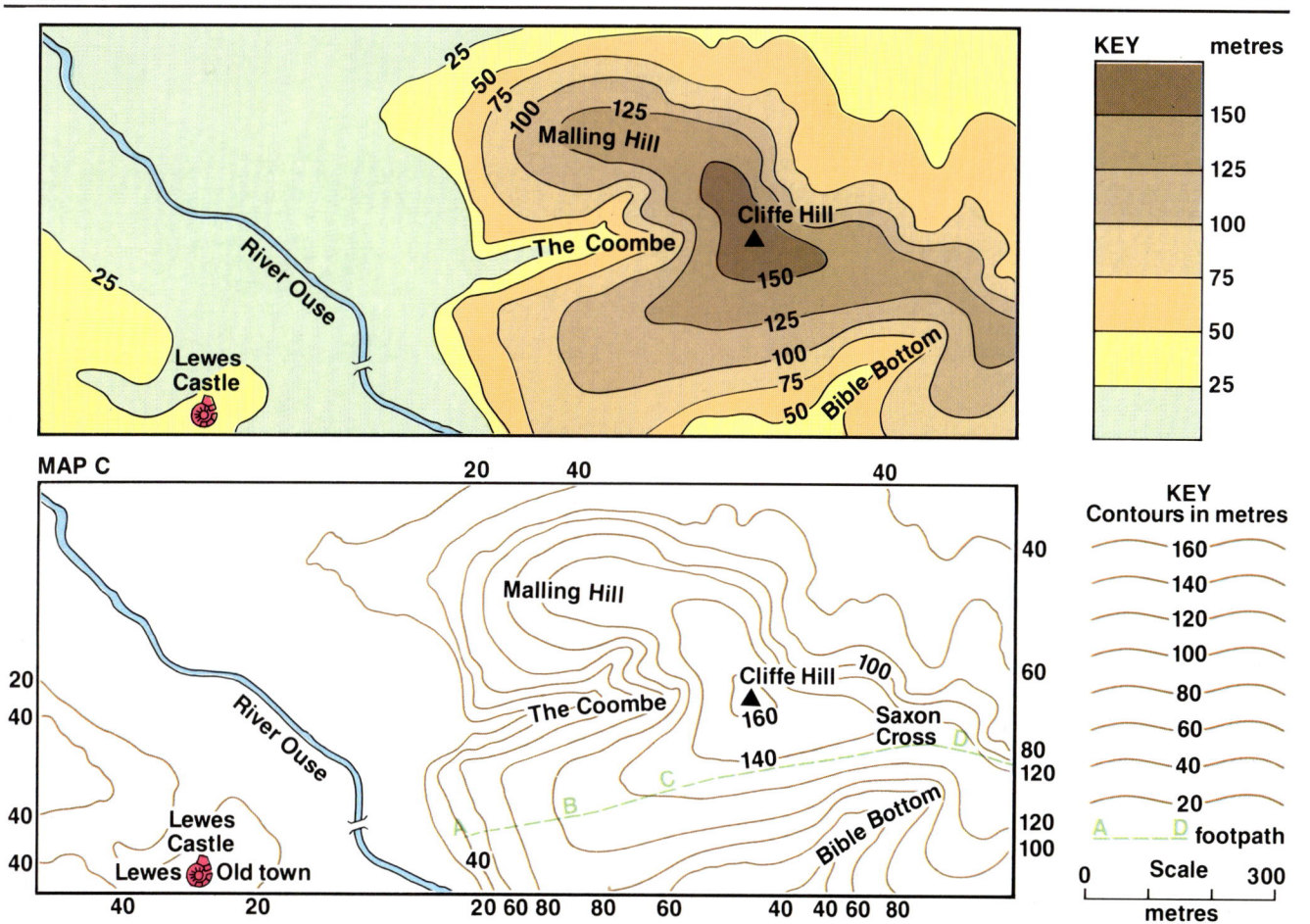

MAP C

KEY metres
- 150
- 125
- 100
- 75
- 50
- 25

KEY Contours in metres
- 160
- 140
- 120
- 100
- 80
- 60
- 40
- 20

A - - - D footpath

Scale 0 — 300 metres

Assignment B

Compare maps B and C.

1. How many layers of colour are shown on map B?
2. How many contours are shown on the key to map B?
3. What is the vertical interval between contours on a) map B b) map C?
4. You are walking along the footpath from A to D.
   The walk is divided into three parts A to B, B to C and C to D. Match these three parts with these descriptions of the slopes:
   (a) The path follows the line of a contour and is almost level.
   (b) The path goes up but not too steeply.
   (c) The path rises steeply up the hill.
   Which was the easiest part of your walk?

One step further B

Look at pictures 1 and 2 showing children standing in rows with their feet at the same level. Can you see how they make human contour lines?

1. In which picture does the human contour show the shape of a valley? Does this contour bend into or out of the higher ground?
2. In which picture does the human contour show the shape of a ridge? Does the contour bend towards or away from the higher ground?
3. Look for shapes of valleys and ridges on maps B and C. Name two valleys and two ridges on the maps.

WEATHER AND CLIMATE

You are going to meet a tall handsome stranger!

Weather forecasting is one way of foreseeing the future. **Weather forecasters** use information about the weather which has been collected for many years. These are **weather records** and they show us patterns in the weather. By collecting rainfall figures for all parts of Britain every year for thirty years they can forecast which places are likely to be wet and which dry. This map shows the average length of sunshine that can be expected each day, from May to October, in Britain. The figures for individual towns are totals for the six months.

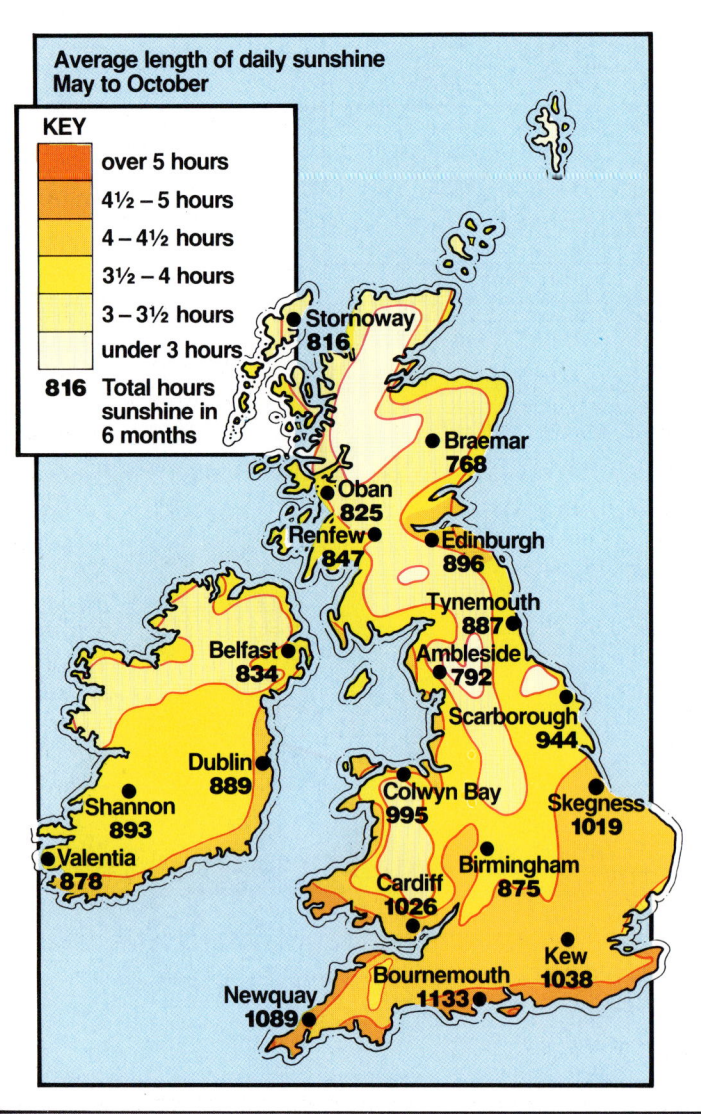

Average length of daily sunshine May to October

KEY
- over 5 hours
- 4½ – 5 hours
- 4 – 4½ hours
- 3½ – 4 hours
- 3 – 3½ hours
- under 3 hours

816 Total hours sunshine in 6 months

- Stornoway 816
- Braemar 768
- Oban 825
- Renfew 847
- Edinburgh 896
- Tynemouth 887
- Belfast 834
- Ambleside 792
- Scarborough 944
- Dublin 889
- Colwyn Bay 995
- Skegness 1019
- Shannon 893
- Birmingham 875
- Valentia 878
- Cardiff 1026
- Kew 1038
- Newquay 1089
- Bournemouth 1133

Assignment A

1 Which area has the most sunshine
   a) England b) Ireland c) Scotland d) Wales?
2 Which area has the least sunshine
   a) England b) Ireland c) Scotland d) Wales?
3 Is there more sunshine in the north or the south of the British Isles?
4 Is the west coast of Ireland more or less sunny than the east coast?
5 Where would you choose for a holiday? Give your reasons.

One step further

Find a physical map of Britain to use with the sunshine map opposite.

1 Find an area of Scotland with low sunshine. Describe the type of land.
2 One part of south-west England receives less sunshine than the rest. What does the physical map tell you about the area?
3 Using the information from questions 1 and 2, what can you predict about the area of low sunshine around Ambleside?
4 Check your prediction by using the physical map.

We may choose a holiday resort because we know that on average it has many hours of sunshine or because it receives enough snow for skiing. We also need much more detailed forecasts. We like to know what the weather will be like tomorrow so that we can plan our activities.

Assignment B

Look at the cartoons.

1. What is the problem in each case?
2. If they had listened to the weather forecast what would each person have heard?
3. What weather conditions does each one need for their activities?
4. Instead of the activities they are attempting what could they have done in these conditions?
5. Draw four cartoons of your own to show other examples of people who do not listen to weather forecasts.

Weather forecasters collect information for their forecasts in a variety of ways.

Satellites orbiting the earth send pictures of weather conditions.

Weather balloons carry an instrument called a **radiosonde** which measures temperature and moisture (water) in the air.

Weather ships report conditions at sea.

Weather stations on land report local conditions.

All this information is sent to **meteorologists** at Bracknell. They are able to build up an overall picture of weather conditions and can forecast what will happen in the near future.

The information is passed to the public in many ways.

WEATHER AND CLIMATE

Winds bring different weather conditions to Britain. Where the wind blows *from* affects our weather.

Winds blowing from the west have crossed the ocean and by the time they reach Britain carry large amounts of water. Winds from the west are usually wet winds.

Personal Research A

Use an atlas to help you with these questions.

1. Which continent will winds have crossed when reaching Britain from the east?
2. Winds from the north have come from the polar area. Is this a cold or warm climate?
3. Winds from the south may have travelled from Africa. Is Africa hotter or colder than Britain?
4. Which ocean do winds from the west cross?

Assignment A

If winds from the south are usually warm and from the east are usually dry, then winds from the south-east will probably be warm dry winds.

1. What type of wind will blow from:
   a) The north-west   b) The south-west
   c) The north-east?
2. What kind of weather might a north-westerly wind bring in winter?
3. In summer the continent of Europe is warm. In winter it is very cold.
   Complete these sentences with the correct endings.

   a) In summer, winds from the east will be — warm and dry. / cold and dry.

   b) In winter, winds from the east will be — warm and dry. / cold and dry.

Assignment B

1. Draw the symbols for:
   a) A temperature of 15°C.
   b) A wind speed of 14 mph from the north-west.
   c) Sunshine.
2. You will need to combine two symbols for the following weather conditions:
   a) Cloudy with sunny periods.
   b) Rain showers with sunny periods.
   c) Sleet (a mixture of rain and snow).
   d) Sunshine with a temperature of 21°C.

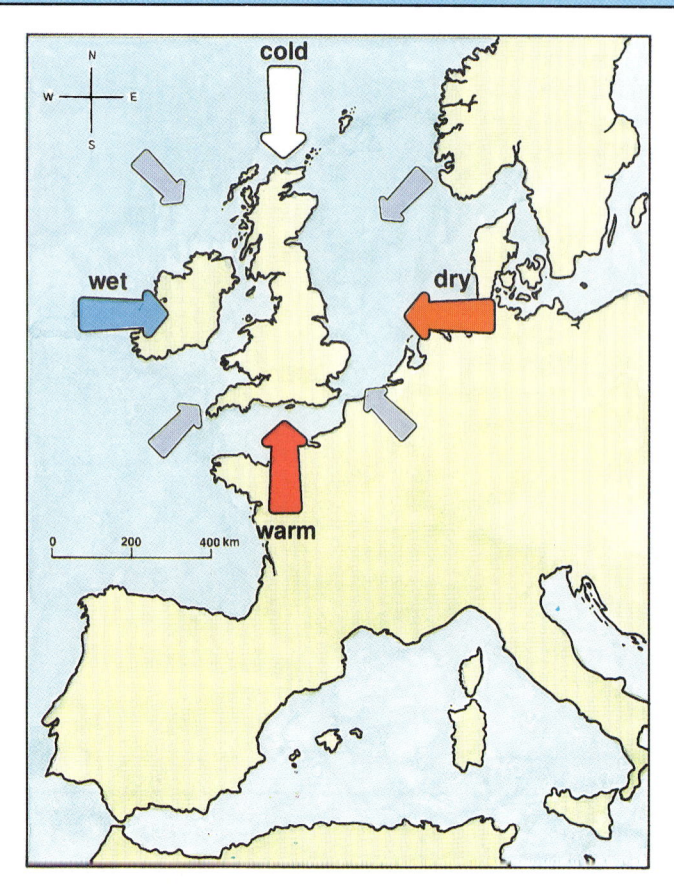

Weather Symbols

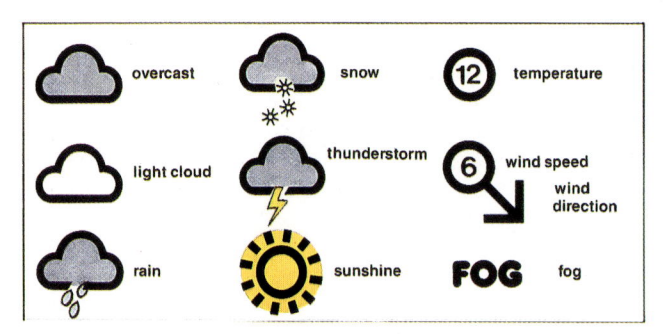

Personal Research B

1. Check whether your answers to question 2 match the symbols used by the T.V. weather forecasters.
2. Compare the symbols used by forecasters on different television channels. Which do you think:
   a) Looks the best.
   b) Explains the weather most clearly.
3. Can you design your own symbols and improve on the T.V. symbols?
4. What is the temperature of freezing point in °C?
5. Draw the symbol for a temperature of -6°C. Choose an appropriate colour.

Tomorrow's Weather

Assignment C

You will need an atlas in order to answer some of these questions.

1. Copy and complete the chart.
2. What time of year do you think this forecast would have been made? Explain your answer.

Area	Symbol	Weather description
N.W. Scotland	☁☔ 11	North westerly wind wet and cool
Lake District		
Tyneside		
Cornwall		
London		
Hull		
Belfast		
Aberystwyth		

One step further A

Sajid wrote this diary for Monday

> It was pouring down when I set off for school. Mum told me to wear my coat. I hate wearing it but today I was glad I took it. Lunchtime was great, we played football in the yard and won 6-5. The puddles had disappeared thanks to the bright sunshine and the breeze. It was dry when I walked home but the sun had gone in, there were no shadows.
> When I left for the Mosque at 4.30 p.m. it was drizzling. I realised I'd left my coat at school! I ran all the way to the Mosque but still got soaked.

1. Draw the pictures in the correct sequence.
2. Draw the appropriate symbols under each picture.
3. Write a similar diary and ask a friend to draw a picture/symbol sequence to go with it.

One step further B

You will need a blank map of the British Isles.

1. Read this weather forecast and draw the appropriate symbols onto the map.

> ❛North and north-east Scotland can expect some severe snowstorms over the next twenty-four hours. There is a chance of the snow drifting, whipped up by winds of 60 or 70 miles an hour.
> Southern Scotland, north and north-west England will be less windy but with sleet showers. The east coast and the south-east of England will stay very cold, maximum temperatures 2°C but remaining dry with sunny spells. Wales, the Midlands and south-west England will be wet with heavy rain spreading westwards throughout the day. The south-west will have the highest temperatures, about 8°C, but enjoy it while you can, snow will be reaching all parts within the next 36 hours.❜

2. What time of year was this forecast made? Explain your answer.
3. Now draw the appropriate symbols for the weather 36 hours later.

47

RIVERS IN FLOOD

Bredon Hill
River Avon
Tewkesbury
River Severn
River Avon
Confluence of the 2 rivers

Assignment A

1. Name the two rivers.
2. What is the weather like?
3. What must the weather have been like before the photo was taken?
4. Which is the main river and which is the **tributary**?
5. Which river is carrying the most mud? How can you tell?
6. What does the word **confluence** mean?

One step further A

1. Where does the rainwater which falls on the Bredon Hills go?
2. Why is Tewkesbury not built on the land between the two rivers?
3. What might happen to the bridges if the river keeps rising?

   How would this affect local people?
4. Find Tewkesbury in an atlas.
   Trace the course of the River Severn.
   Where does it reach the sea?

A Near the source of the River Severn

Reasons for flooding
- Heavy rain over the hills
- Melting snow and heavy rain
- A high tide and heavy rain
- Farmers laying new drains
- Trees, which bind soil and soak up water, are cut down.

FLOOD CONTROL

One step further B

1 Why do farmers want their fields to drain more quickly?
2 How does this affect the amount of water entering rivers?
3 In what season will floods caused by melting snow occur?
4 Will high tides cause flooding either
   a) near an estuary   or   b) near a source?

B Clywedog Dam

C Thames Barrier

Assignment B

Look at photo A

1 Are the valley sides steep or gentle?
2 What has been planted? How might this slow the water entering the stream?

Look at photo B

3 What has been built across the River Severn? How does this help to prevent floods further down river?
4 Imagine you live down river. Write a story of the day the dam burst.

Look at photo C

5 Which city is this?
6 How do you think the barrier works?
7 When would the barrier be used?
8 What might happen if this city were flooded?
9 Why was a dam not built here?

NORTH WALES: FIELDWORK

Sally and Sajid's class are in North Wales for field study work. They are staying in a converted farmhouse near Tal-y-Bont in the Conwy valley midway between Conwy and Betws-y-Coed.

On Sunday evening Mr Ellis showed the children a map of the area and they discussed the places they would visit and what they would do there.

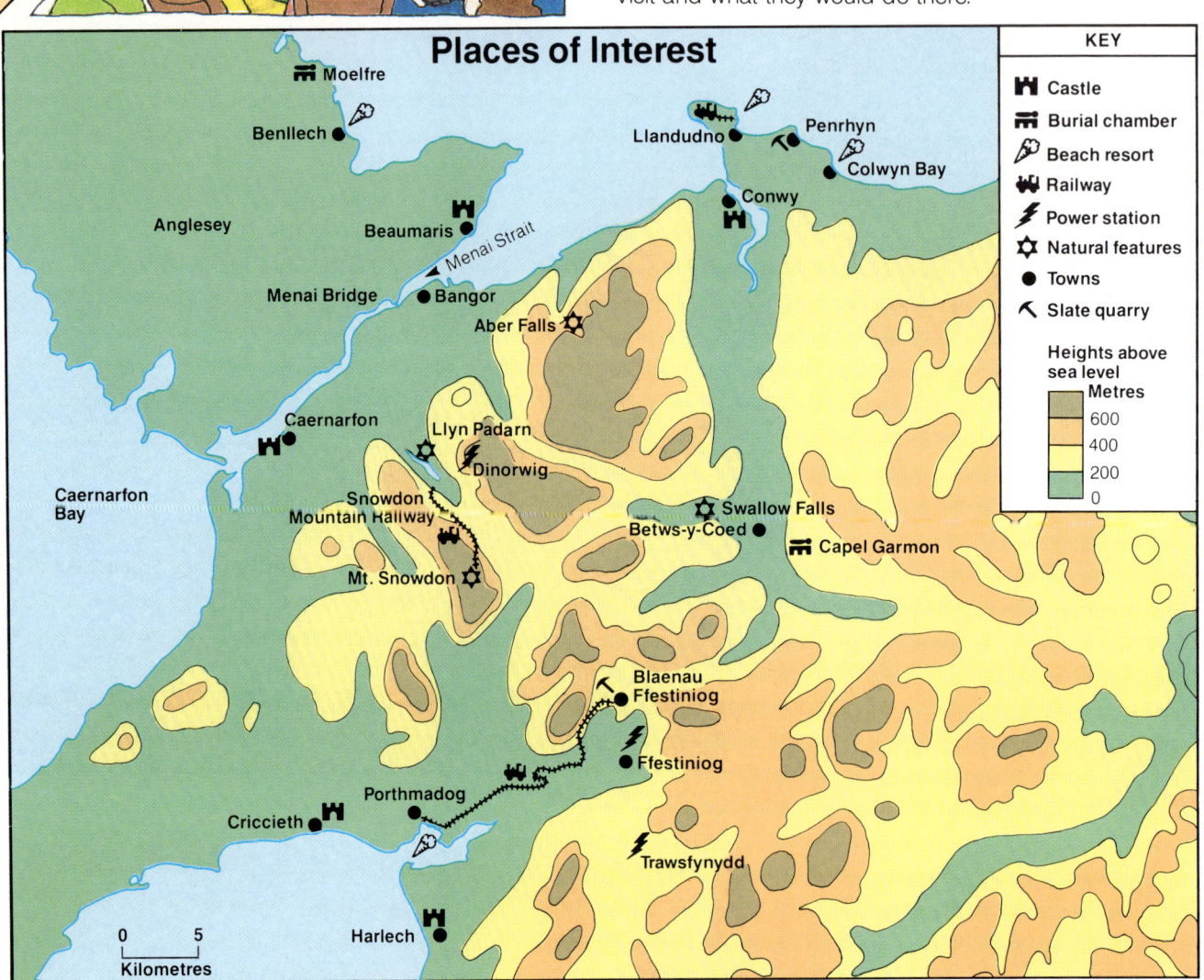

Places of Interest

KEY
- Castle
- Burial chamber
- Beach resort
- Railway
- Power station
- Natural features
- Towns
- Slate quarry

Heights above sea level
Metres
- 600
- 400
- 200
- 0

Assignment A

1. Copy and complete the chart.
2. Rearrange this list of places putting the highest first and the lowest last: Llandudno, Snowdon, Blaenau Ffestiniog, and Aber Falls.
3. What feature is common in the location of all the castles shown?
4. Can you suggest reasons why?

Interest	Location	Essential Weather
Mining	Penrhyn	Any
Ancient tombs		
Seashells		
	Caernarfon	
		Sunshine
Power		
	Mt. Snowdon	
Steam trains		
	Aber Falls	

Assignment B

The class travel by minibus to a different destination each day. They begin each journey at Tal-y-Bont. The minibus averages 40 km an hour.

This is a record Sajid kept of a journey from Tal-y-Bont to Capel Curig.

Destination	Route	Approx. distance	Time
Capel Curig	B5106 South to Betws-y-Coed then A5 West to Capel Curig	20 km	30 mins.

Make similar records for the following destinations: Conwy, Colwyn Bay, Blaenau Ffestiniog, Llangefni, Harlech, and Llyn Trawsfyndd.

One step further

1 Using the two maps draw similar records for destinations chosen for these purposes:
   a) To cross the Menai Bridge and visit a burial chamber.
   b) To travel on a steam train which departs from a beach resort.
   c) To visit a power station and paddle in Llyn Padarn.
   d) To look at Caernarfon Bay and the Menai Strait from a castle tower.

2 The minibus dropped the children on the B5106 so they could walk along the Roman Road to Aber. The walk took three hours.
   a) Find the distance of the journey.
   b) What speed did the children average?
   c) Which route did the minibus take?
   d) How long did it take?
   e) How long did the minibus wait for the children?

NORTH WALES: FARMING

Mr Evans, a local farmer, stopped to talk to Sally and Sajid.

Sally and Sajid's class stayed in this former farmhouse called Bron-y-Gader.

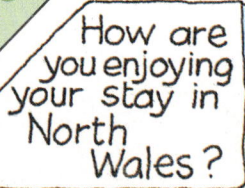

How are you enjoying your stay in North Wales?

It's great! But it's very different from home.

There's no electricity and we get water straight from the hillside.

We have to take turns emptying the chemical toilet and it's my turn tonight!

Well it's nice to see people living in the farmhouse again

Why do you say that?

When I was a boy these hills had many families living in farmhouses like this. Now there are only a few of us left.

They must have been very sorry to leave such a beautiful place.

I'm going to ring home tomorrow, there's so much to tell everyone!

Assignment A

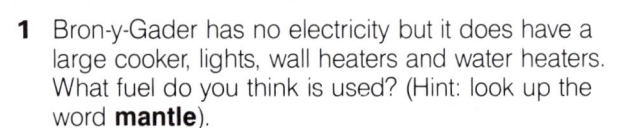

1. Bron-y-Gader has no electricity but it does have a large cooker, lights, wall heaters and water heaters. What fuel do you think is used? (Hint: look up the word **mantle**).
2. How do you think the fuel is delivered, stored and used? There are no pipelines leading to Bron-y-Gader.
3. These are Sajid's plans of what he would do when he arrived at Bron-y-Gader. Some of them proved impossible. What could he not do? Why?

> **My plans**
> When I get to the farmhouse I'm going to get a bunk next to the light switch, then I can switch on at night if I hear any noises - like people snoring or the toilet flushing. I'll unpack and watch some T.V. until the meal is ready. I've got a radio alarm clock, so I'm going to be the first awake every morning.

One step further A

1. How would your day be affected if you had no electricity?
2. Look at the photograph above.
   a) Can you suggest why the farmhouse is made of these materials?
   b) Compare Bron-y-Gader with your home (think about materials and style). List the similarities and differences.
3. The families who once lived in these farmhouses could no longer earn their living from farming. Why did they not continue to live in the house and find other jobs on the hillsides?

   Where do you think they moved to, towns or other rural areas? Explain your answer.
4. Compare this movement with that of the Sudras and the Patels earlier in this book. What similarities are there?

Mr Evans showed the children some photographs and described his year on the farm.

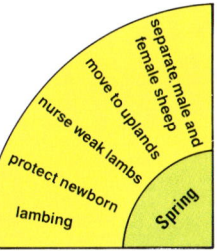

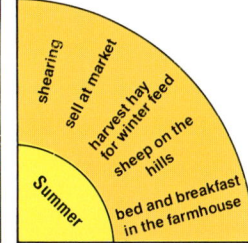

Spring: lambing, protect newborn, nurse weak lambs, move to uplands, separate male and female sheep

Summer: shearing, sell at market, harvest hay for winter feed, sheep on the hills, bed and breakfast in the farmhouse

Autumn: sell at market, mating, dipping to kill ticks

Winter: move weaker ewes to lowland, rescue sheep in heavy snow, feed hill sheep

A The new born lamb must be protected from crows which will eat its eyes and tongue if allowed near.

The sheep need to be moved from high to lowland and back again depending on the season.

B Male (wether) lambs are fed on good grass—they are fattened up ready to be sold for meat.

C The shearer travels from farm to farm. The work is hard.

For most lambs the final destination is the auction market followed by the abbatoir.

Assignment B

1. a) What dangers are there for a newly born lamb?
   b) How can a farmer protect them?
2. Why are sheep sheared every year?
3. How does the farmer control so many sheep on the hillside or along a road?
4. What evidence is there in photo A that this lamb has just been born?
5. a) Shearing like that in photo C could not have taken place at Bron-y-Gader. Why not?
   b) What kind of shears must they have used in the past?
6. Would shearing in the past have been quicker?
7. What effect has electric shearing made on the number of people employed? Explain your answer.

Personal Research

1. Find out whether there are:
   a) Empty farmhouses in your area.
   b) Farmhouses which are now lived in by people who are not farmers.
2. Can you discover where the farming people have moved to, and where the newcomers work?

One step further B

1. Most of the male lambs are sold for slaughter after six months. Many of the females are kept.
   a) Why are only a few males kept?
   b) What will the females be used for?
2. Why do farmers mark their sheep with a distinctive colour dye?

NUCLEAR SHOCK

Lamb ban in 2 areas after radiation fear

The Government has announced a three-week ban on the movement and slaughter of sheep within Cumbria and North Wales, after the discovery of increased levels of radioactivity in the wake of the Chernobyl nuclear disaster in the Soviet Union.

An estimated 5,000 flocks, comprising about 1,250,000 ewes and lambs, will be affected by the restrictions.

"1986 was a bad year for North Wales sheep farmers. We weren't allowed to sell our lambs. Many of us thought we would be ruined."

The mood among Welsh farmers was sombre. Mr Jack Jones at Gwynedd, said "I am very frightened for the future. If sheep farming is our life. If this land becomes poisoned, it would kill off farming in North Wales for ever."

Mrs Enid Williams, in the same area, said: "The end of June and July is our busiest period for selling lambs. We are terribly worried, as this could drive us into debt."

An official of the Meat and Livestock Commission said, "Clearly people are going to be concerned about the safety of what they eat."

On April 25th 1986 a major accident occurred at Chernobyl in Ukraine (then in the Soviet Union). A nuclear reactor was destroyed in a fire and a cloud of radioactive gas was released. The cloud passed over Britain on May 3rd, 4th and 5th. Some parts of Britain received heavy rainfall during those three days and radioactivity was brought down to earth from the cloud by rain. Parts of Scotland, Cumbria and North Wales were the worst affected areas.

£1.96 per lb — MAY 1ST 1986
99p per lb — JUNE 23RD 1986

Assignment A

Mr Evans told Sajid and Sally that 1986 was a year when many sheep farmers feared ruin.

1. Why did the Government ban the movement of sheep in North Wales?
2. Why was there no ban on sheep movement and slaughter in eastern England?
3. If farmers cannot sell lambs how does this affect their income?
4. What happened to the price of lamb between May 1st and the end of June?
5. The Government said all meat on sale was safe, but many people stopped buying lamb. Why do you think people acted in this way?

Nuclear power is a *controversial* issue. People feel strongly about the subject. Here are statements made about nuclear energy.

New jobs created • No Smoke • Mining jobs lost • Nuclear Waste • Conserves fossil fuels • CHEAP • Can be used for weapons • RADIOACTIVE LEAKS

This table shows the percentage of electricity generated by nuclear power in the countries of the E.C.

	%
Belgium	65
Denmark	0
Eire	0
France	70
Greece	0
Italy	5
Luxembourg	0
Netherlands	6
Portugal	0
Spain	32
U.K.	20
Germany	32

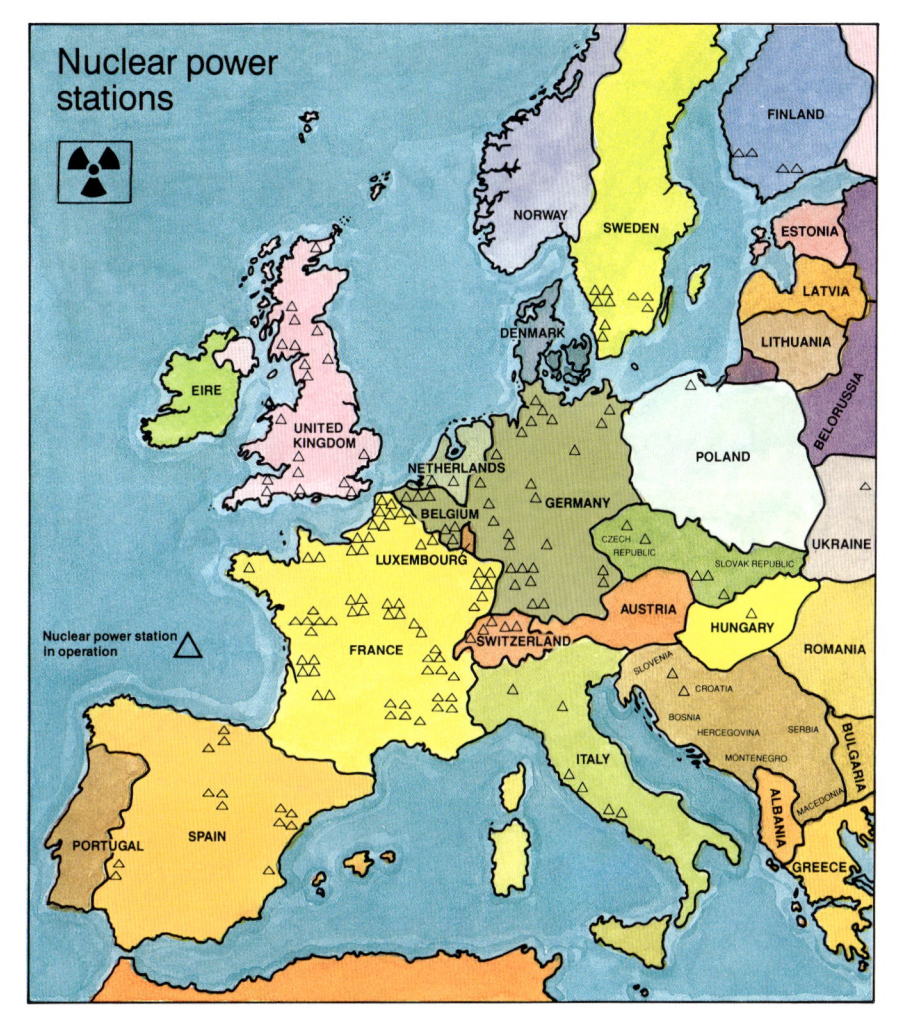

Nuclear power stations

One step further

1. Why is Mr Evans so strongly opposed to nuclear power stations?

2. a) Look at the statements on nuclear power. Divide them into two groups, those in favour and those against.
   b) Compare your list with a friend's. Do you agree?

3. a) List the countries of Europe, shown on the map, which are not in the E.C.
   b) Which have nuclear power?
   c) Which do not?

Assignment B

1. Sweden plans to close all its nuclear power stations by the year 2010. Why do you think this decision has been taken?

2. France has very little coal, and has no oil or gas of its own.
   a) What other sources of power could France develop besides nuclear power?
   b) If you were in the French Government which sources of power would you vote for?

3. It is sometimes said that nuclear power will make tomorrow's problems for today's children. Discuss in groups what you think this means.
   Do you agree with it or not?

Personal Research

Sally told Mr Evans that acid rain pollution is caused by coal and oil-fired power stations.
Find out what acid rain is, how it spreads, its effects on the environment, and which countries are affected.

OIL AND GAS

All these oil and gas fields have been discovered since the Dutch found natural gas deep in rocks under the north of their country in 1959.

Oil and Gas Fields and Pipelines

KEY

- — · — · Boundaries in the North Sea ownership of gas and oil
- Gasfields
- Oilfields
- Gas pipeline
- Oil pipeline
- Gas terminal

Important gasfields

- F Frigg
- S Schlockteren
- R Rough
- W West Sole
- V Viking
- I Indefatigable
- L Leman
- H Hewett
- M Morecambe Bay

Important oilfields

- B Brent
- Fo Forties
- E Ekofisk
- C Claymore
- Be Beatrice
- Ma Magnus

Oil and natural gas were formed from the bodies of tiny creatures which lived in the sea millions of years ago.

Some of the oil and gas is in rocks only 900 metres below the sea bed, but sometimes the depths can be much greater, 2000 metres and more. Drilling for gas or oil in water is more expensive than drilling on land. The deeper it has to be drilled, and the further it has to be pumped to the shore, the more expensive it is. The water in the south of the North Sea is less deep than in the north.

There is probably enough oil and gas in the rocks around Britain to supply needs for 30 years.

A

B

Look at the photos of the men who do the drilling. They are called **roustabouts**. They have to work in all weathers and the work is very dangerous. The sections of the drilling gear are very heavy, each section of drill pipe can weigh 100 tonnes. The sharp teeth of the drilling bit cut down through the rock to reach the oil or gas (photo A).

Gas and oil are pumped through pipelines to the shore. The oil goes to oil refineries to be made into petrol, diesel, chemicals and plastics. The gas is cleaned. Gas is given a smell at terminals, natural gas has no smell. The gas goes through very large pipes to towns and cities where it is put into smaller yellow plastic pipes which feed gas to houses, offices and factories.

Assignment

1. Name a gasfield
   a) on the boundary between Britain and Norway.
   b) linked by pipeline to Easington terminal.
   c) in the Netherlands.
2. Which British gas terminal has the largest number of gas pipes coming ashore?
3. Name three major cities which are served by the gas pipeline network.
4. Name an oil refinery and a gas terminal in Scotland.
5. Where does the oil which is refined in Tees-side come from?
6. Name a country other than Britain which has a large amount of oil and gas in its part of the North Sea.
7. What work does a roustabout do?
   Why is it a well paid job?
   Why is it dangerous?
8. Describe what a drilling bit looks like and its purpose.

One step further

1. Why is a smell added to natural gas?
2. List the factors which make oil/gas exploration expensive.
3. Which area would be the most expensive to operate in, the northern sector of the North Sea or the southern sector? Give your reasons.

Personal Research

1. If your local area is supplied with natural gas find out when the supply was provided.
2. Are there areas where natural gas will never be piped (think about physical/population factors)?
3. What kind of gas was used before natural gas was piped to Britain?

ON A RIG

Assignment A

Look at the artist's drawing of two rigs in the North Sea: West Sole and Magnus. From the information on this page, and the previous two pages, answer these questions:

1. How deep is the sea water at West Sole platform?
2. How deep is the water at Magnus?
3. How does the depth of water at Magnus compare with the height of the British Telecom tower?
4. Which platform is for gas and which for oil and gas?
5. Which platform is in the North Sea?
6. Why did the Magnus rig cost more than the West Sole?

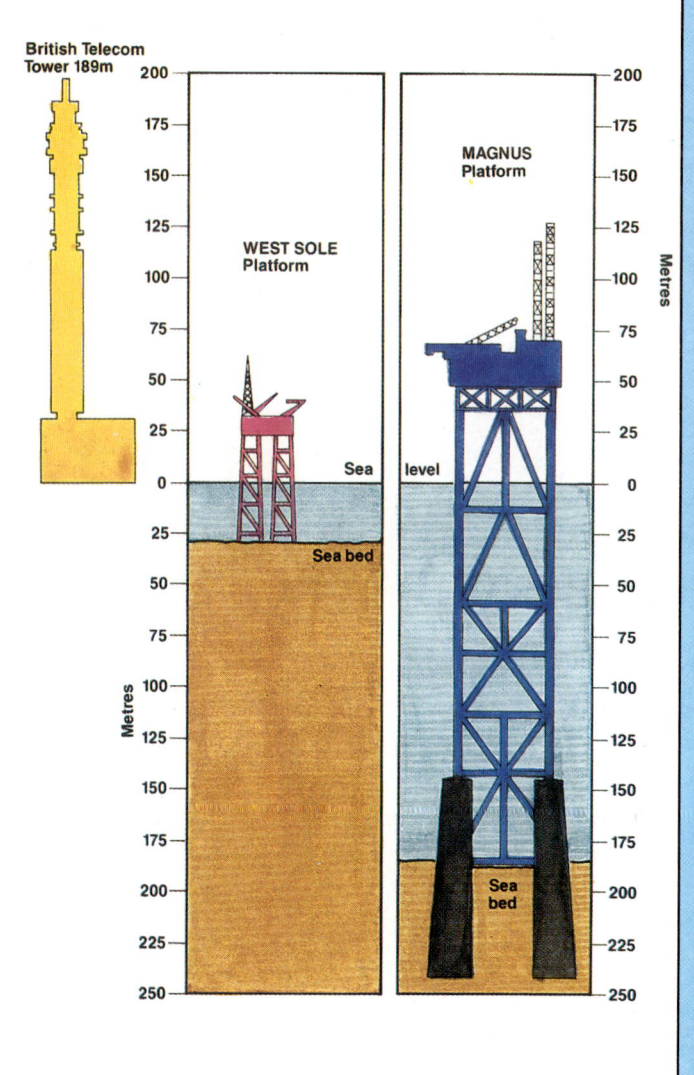

One step further A

Look at the photo of the British Gas platform at the Leman gas field.

1. What is the flat surface marked 'H' used for?
2. Which of these platforms has the gas drilling rig and the accommodation?
3. Name two ways supplies can be brought to the rig
4. How are the platforms joined?
5. Draw a picture of the Leman platform in a storm.
6. Imagine there is a heavy storm with strong winds in this part of the North Sea and one of the crew has an accident. Describe your feelings if you were:
   a) the member of crew injured.
   b) the helicopter pilot.
   c) one of the family at home.

USING OIL AND GAS

Look at the graph which shows how world oil prices have changed sharply in recent years. Oil prices rise when there is a demand for oil, but not enough oil to meet it. Oil prices fall when there is a glut of oil due to oil producing countries exporting more than is needed.

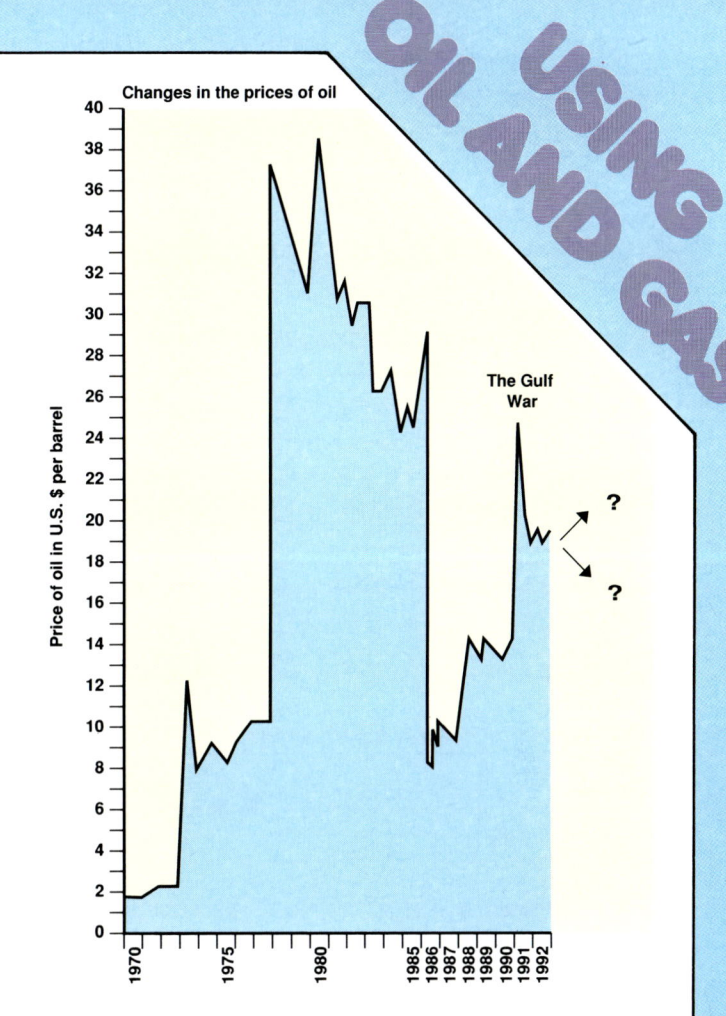

Assignment B

1. In which years did world oil prices rise rapidly?
2. When did world oil prices fall sharply?
3. What causes oil prices to change up or down?
4. Small cars which do not use much petrol became popular in the 1970s. Why?

One step further B

1. Discuss with your friends and your teacher what will happen in the future if
   a) oil prices increase?
   b) oil prices decrease?
   c) the world begins to run out of oil and gas?
2. How might this affect decisions about nuclear power?
3. What do we mean when we say oil is a non-renewable fuel?

How gas is used.

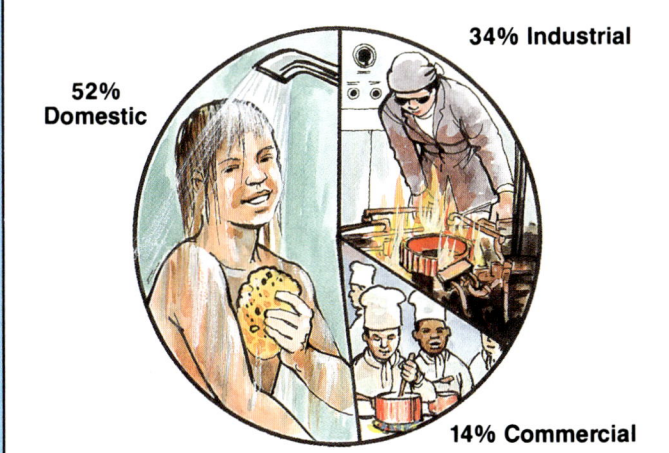

52% Domestic
34% Industrial
14% Commercial

How oil is used.

Assignment C

1. List the uses of gas in the home.
2. Discuss with friends and your teacher what people consider to be the advantages of gas over other fuels.
3. List the forms of transport which use oil products as a fuel.

Personal Research

1. Try to discover the location of power stations which use oil or gas as a fuel. Why do you think they are located at these particular points?
2. Are there any industries in your area which use gas. Who might you contact to find out?
3. Oil is used in a wide variety of products. List as many as you can that are in everyday use in the home.

VOLCANOES AND EARTHQUAKES

What happens to porridge and rice pudding after they have been cooked? They form a skin on top, while still hot underneath. The surface of the world is like that. It is made of a rocky skin or crust of lighter rocks, floating on heavy hot liquid rock underneath. We call the slabs of light crust **plates**.

In some places the plates are moving apart. The North American plate is moving away from the Eurasian plate at the rate of 2 centimetres a year. The gap is filled by hot volcanic rock from below.

In other places the plates are slowly crashing into each other. At these places the plates crumple up and one is slowly destroyed. The heat given off produces violent earthquakes and big volcanoes.

On Map A the arrows show in which direction the plates are moving. Some plates break up into smaller plates. Earthquakes are caused by rocks cracking, being torn apart or crushed together. We call these cracks in the rocks **faults**. Big earthquakes can destroy buildings and roads. Volcanoes are mainly found along fault lines in the rocks usually close to the edge of the plates.

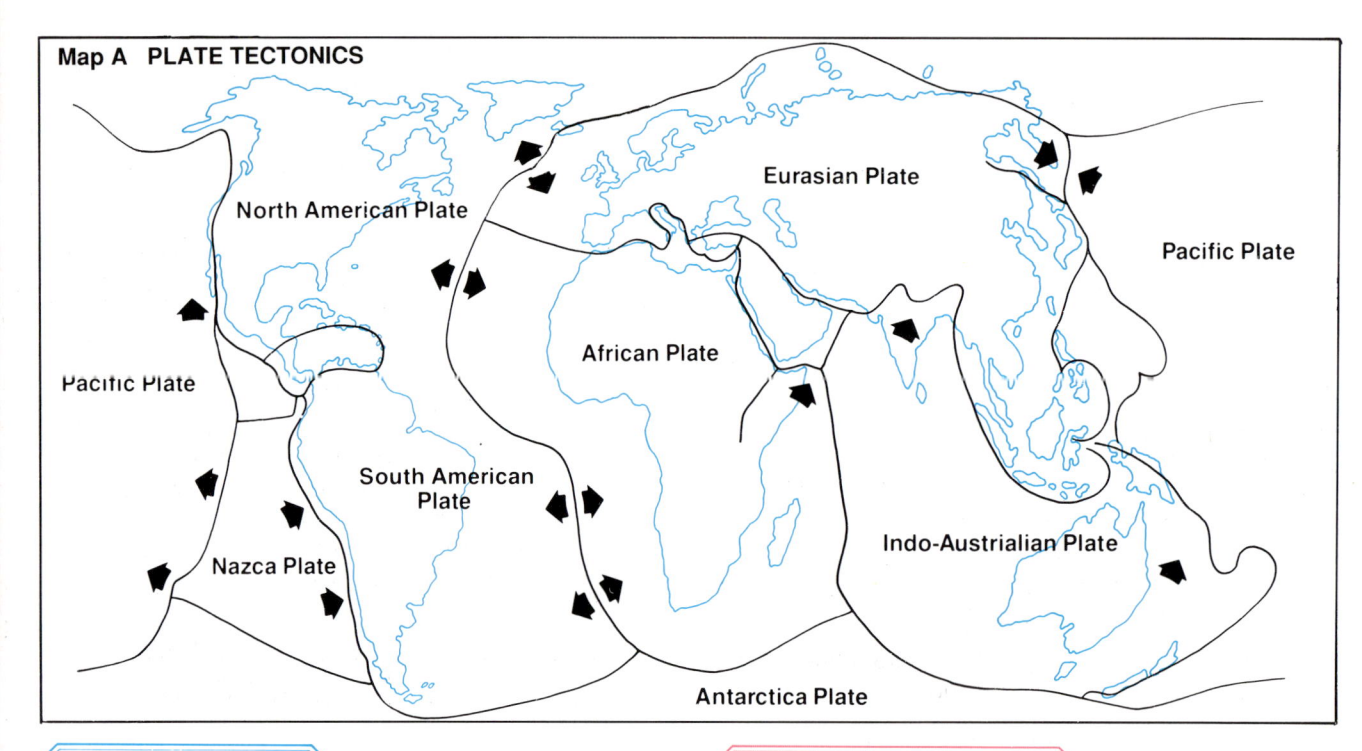

Map A PLATE TECTONICS

Assignment

1. Name two plates which are moving apart.
2. Name two plates which are moving together.
3. What causes (a) earthquakes and (b) volcanoes?
4. Why are earthquakes and volcanoes mainly found in the same areas?
5. Name an island with many volcanoes.
6. Which part of Africa has a large number of volcanoes?

One step further A

1. Use an atlas to complete the chart. One has been done for you.
2. What similarities are there between the names of continents and the names of plates?

City	Country	Continent	Plate
Lima			
Sydney			
Nairobi			
New York			
Madras	India	Asia	Indo-Australian
Moscow			
Brasilia			
Belfast			

Map B   VOLCANOES AND EARTHQUAKE ZONES

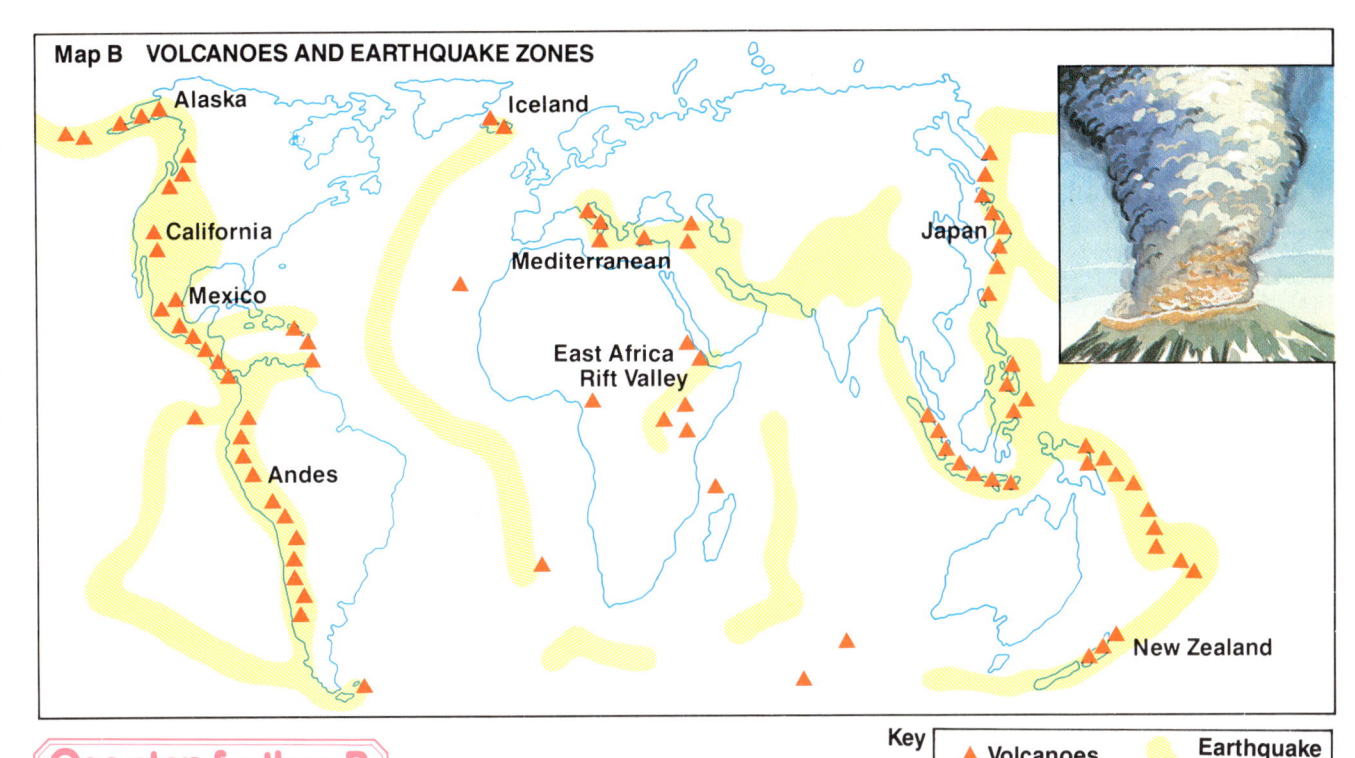

Key: ▲ Volcanoes   Earthquake zones

One step further B

Photograph A shows earthquake damage in San Francisco in 1989.

1. Imagine you and your family are caught in an earthquake.
   Describe what it feels like during the earthquake and what happens afterwards.

2. Imagine you are a rescue worker in a city after an earthquake. What did you do? Why were you frightened during the rescue?

3. If you owned the building in the picture, what would you expect from the Government?

4. Why do people still want to live in cities which have dreadful earthquakes?

5. Would you feel safer in a block of flats or on the streets during an earthquake? Give your reasons.

Personal Research

1. Photo B show the ruins of a city in South Italy which was destroyed by a volcano in AD 79. Find out what happened. Which volcano did the damage? How do we know so much about life in the city so long ago? What was the name of the city?

2. Find out what happened in Lisbon in 1755.

3. What happened in San Francisco on April 18th, 1906?

A

B

61

CHECKPOINT: THE WORLD

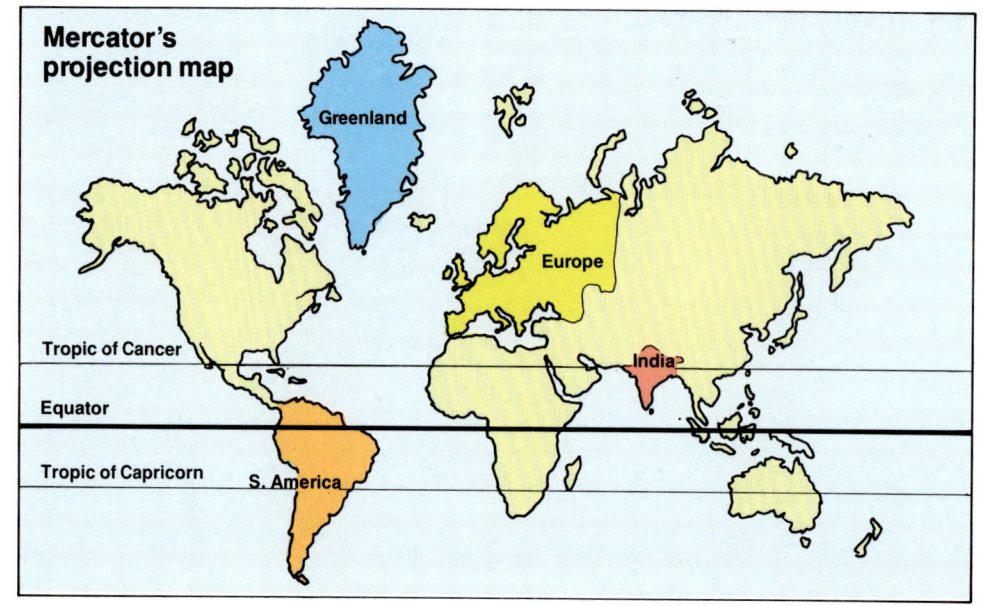

Mercator's projection map

- Greenland
- Europe
- India
- S. America
- Tropic of Cancer
- Equator
- Tropic of Capricorn

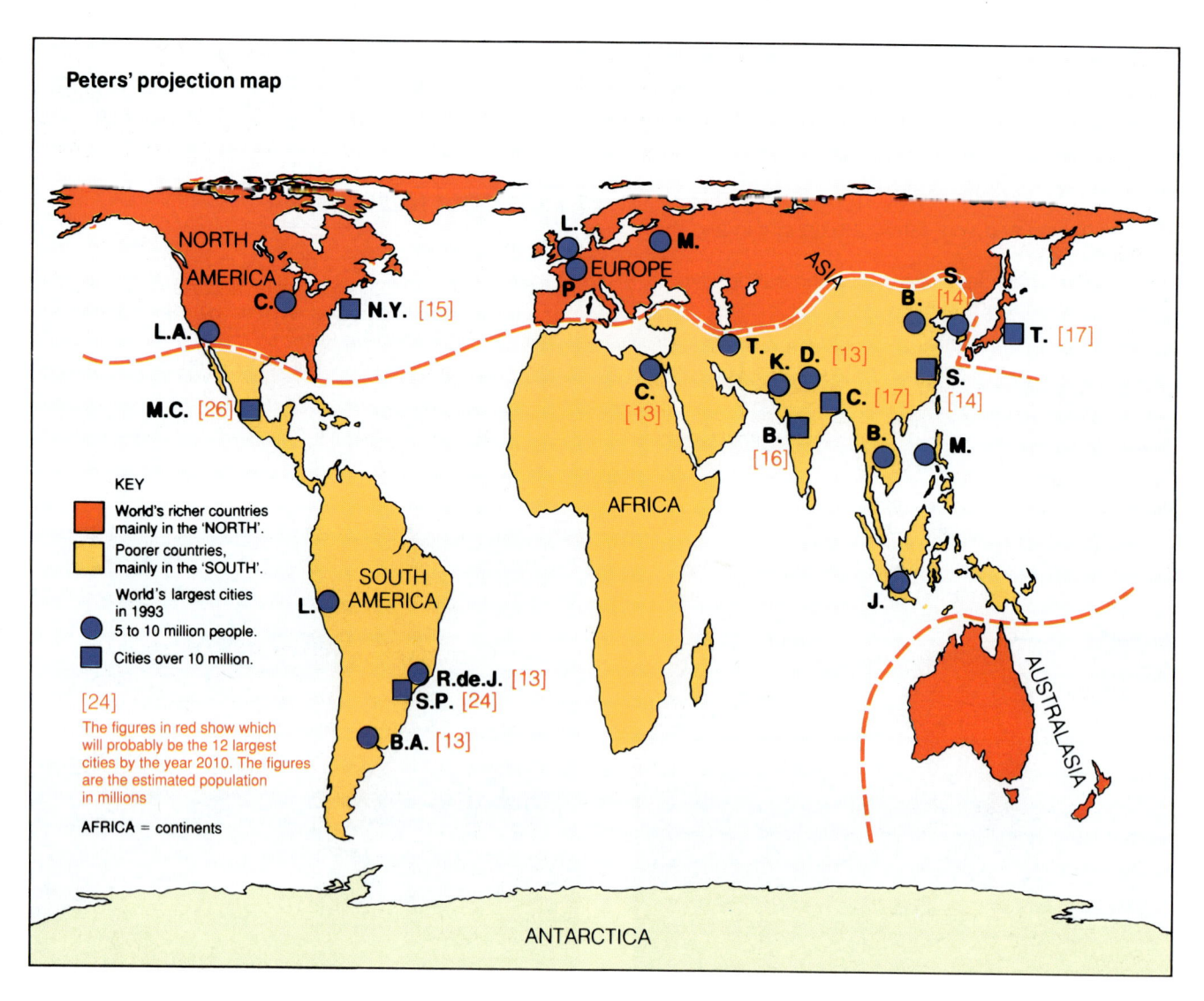

Peters' projection map

NORTH AMERICA
- L.
- M.
- P. EUROPE
- C.
- L.A.
- N.Y. [15]
- M.C. [26]
- C. [13]
- T.
- K. D. [13]
- B. [16]
- B.
- C. [17]
- S. [14]
- B. [14]
- S. [14]
- T. [17]
- M.
- J.
- ASIA
- AFRICA
- SOUTH AMERICA
- L.
- R.de.J. [13]
- S.P. [24]
- B.A. [13]
- AUSTRALASIA
- ANTARCTICA

KEY
- World's richer countries mainly in the 'NORTH'.
- Poorer countries, mainly in the 'SOUTH'.
- World's largest cities in 1993
- ● 5 to 10 million people.
- ■ Cities over 10 million.

[24] The figures in red show which will probably be the 12 largest cities by the year 2010. The figures are the estimated population in millions

AFRICA = continents

The large map shows the 24 largest cities in the world. In many richer countries the population of cities is falling. People are moving out of cities to smaller towns and villages.

In the poorer parts of the world the opposite is happening. Many people are moving from the countryside to live in the big cities. For example, Mexico City had 5 million people in 1965. What is the estimate of its population in the year 2010?

Assignment A

1. Using your atlas and map, make a list of the world's 24 largest cities by completing this table:

Large City	Country	Continent
L. London	U.K	Europe
P. Paris		

2. Which were the four largest cities in the world in 1993?
3. Which two cities will probably be the biggest in 2010?
4. How many of the world's 12 largest cities in 2010 will be in a) the poorer countries b) the richer countries?

Have you ever thought of how the round world is made to fit on a flat map?
Look at the two world maps opposite.
The large map was drawn by Peters in 1973. This shows all land areas according to their size. It is called an **equal area map.**
The small map was drawn by Mercator in 1569. It makes countries towards the North Pole seem much larger than they really are.

Assignment B

1. Compare these maps with a globe. How accurate are they?
2. Which looks larger on **Mercator's map**, Greenland or India? Which really is larger?
3. Which looks larger on Mercator's map, Europe or South America? Which is larger?
4. Why does the **Peters' map** look a bit odd compared with the globe?

A

B

All city centres have problems with traffic and pollution. Look at photos A and B. One shows Delhi, the other shows a street in Bangkok.

One step further

1. Discuss with your friends which photo shows a street in Delhi and which is Bangkok. Write down the reasons for your choice.
2. Write two sentences comparing the traffic problems in Bangkok and Delhi.
3. What sort of pollution is a problem in Bangkok?

A GREENER WORLD GAME

FINISH

FINISH	33	32 You leave dangerous litter in the countryside	31 Step in dog's mess. Miss a turn.	30	
24 Bottle Bank	25 You collect aluminium cans for recycling.	26 The beach is polluted so you can't go for a swim.	27	28 Acid rain is killing trees	29 OZONE
23	22 I eat paper	21 You have made a bird box for your garden.	20	19 You go out and leave tv switched on	18
12 You make a compost bin to recycle organic waste.	13	14 You leave the tap running in the toilets.	15	16	17
11 You switch off lights in the classrooms.	10	9	8 You help plant trees in school grounds.	7	6 You start a 'green club' at school. Recycled paper
START	2 Cut foot on broken glass. Miss a turn	2	3	4 You help school make a pond and wildlife garden.	5 Can Bank

This is an environmental snakes and ladders game using dice and counters.

As you play the game, discuss each idea with your friends.

£4.50

CONTENTS

GARY LINEKER	6
DEAN SAUNDERS	10
ALLY McCOIST	12
TEDDY SHERINGHAM	14
DAVID PLATT	16
NIGEL CLOUGH	18
IAN WRIGHT	20
MO JOHNSTON	22
ALAN SMITH	24
NIALL QUINN	26
PETER BEARDSLEY	28
JOHN BARNES	30
TONY COTTEE	32
STEVE BULL	34
PAUL GASCOIGNE	36
BRIAN DEANE	38
KERRY DIXON	40
MARK HUGHES	42
MARCO GABBIADINI	44
ROY WEGERLE	46
MATTHEW LE TISSIER	48
LEE CHAPMAN	50
BRIAN McCLAIR	52
IAN RUSH	54
HUGO SANCHEZ	56
MARCO VAN BASTEN	57
JURGEN KLINSMANN	58
GIANLUCA VIALLI	59
LOTHAR MATTHAUS	60
ROBERTO BAGGIO	61

Copyright © 1991 Performance Entertainment Ltd. All rights reserved.
Published in Great Britain by World International Publishing Ltd., an Egmont Company, Egmont House, PO Box 111, Great Ducie Street, Manchester M60 3BL. Printed in Italy.
All photographs are by Coloursport.
ISBN 0-7498-0403-3

Welcome to **STRIKER**. I hope you will enjoy reading about some of the most talented and prolific goalscorers in the game today.

During my soccer career, I have had the privilege of playing alongside some of the most talented strikers in the business, both at club and international level and have great respect for the many and varied skills of these great players. Whether in the League, Europe or the World arena, there is no greater thrill for a football supporter than the sight of an expertly executed goal.

Each season, exciting new players emerge, some having worked their way through the apprentice ranks to take their first team place in top flight football, others improving steadily until reaching peak form. In fact, there are so many up and coming strikers, as well as a wealth of established names, that it has been impossible to include every notable goalscorer in these pages, but I hope the balance of newcomers and star players is a fair reflection of British and overseas talent.

A great striker has a combination of speed, balance, ball control, and often the knack of creating chances from impossible situations and ultimately finishing with the ball in the back of the net. But football is a team game and all strikers depend on good service from midfield and a good defence to control the opposing forward line. The goalscorer gets the credit, but the skills of the rest of his team-mates are equally important.

Whoever you support, I hope you find some of your favourite players in this book and I'm sure you will join me in looking forward to many more spectacular goals from these masters of their craft in the future.

Best wishes,

Gary Lineker

GARY LINEKER

Currently one of England's best-loved and most prolific goalscorers, Lineker was born on 30 November 1960 and began his career with his home-town club, Leicester City, where he started as an apprentice. He made his League debut against Oldham on 1 January 1979, but did not return to the first team until the end of the season. He remained at City from 1977-85 and scored a total of 95 League goals. During 1981-2, he established his regular first team place and was City's top scorer for the next three seasons, with 26, 22 and 24 goals respectively.

Gary's England career began in May 1984 when they met Scotland in a 1-1 draw. Ironically, he did not score his first goal for his country until his sixth match when he netted two goals in the 5-0 win against the USA, a year after his debut. Since then, he has gone on to prove he is amongst the world's top strikers and in the 1986 World Cup he emerged as the tournament's leading scorer. He netted a total of six goals including a hat-trick against Poland.

In 1985, Lineker moved to Everton for £800,000 and scored 30 League goals in his first and only season with the club. He was a sensation at Goodison Park and Everton finished runners-up to Liverpool in both the League and the FA Cup. In the same season, Gary was awarded both the PFA and FWA Player of the Year awards.

Gary left the English League in 1986, when Barcelona and Terry Venables stepped in to sign him, after his tremendous World Cup performance, in a £2.75 million deal. He did equally well in Spain and continued to net goals. He won a Spanish Cup-winners medal in 1988, but was sold soon after Johan Cruyff joined the Barcelona management, despite huge protests from the fans. It was Terry Venables, now Managing Director of Spurs, who once again signed Lineker, for a fee of £1.2 million.

Back in the English League, Gary's prolific goalscoring continued and during 1989-90 he scored 24 League goals in 38 appearances. Gary's ability to score goals is founded on his lightning turn of speed and he is an outstanding finisher, equally accurate with either foot or his head.

In the 1990 World Cup, he played in all seven matches and scored four goals. In England's first game against the Republic of Ireland he scored after just eight minutes and in the quarter-final, against Cameroon, he scored two penalties in England's 3-2 victory. In the semi-final against West Germany, Gary scored the equaliser but England lost the match 4-3 on penalties. Gary is on course to be England's greatest goalscorer in history. On England's 1991 summer tour of Australia, New Zealand and Malaysia, Gary overtook Jimmy Greaves' tally of 44 goals for England. With England well placed to qualify for the European Championships in 1992, Charlton's record of 49 goals for England is in his sights.

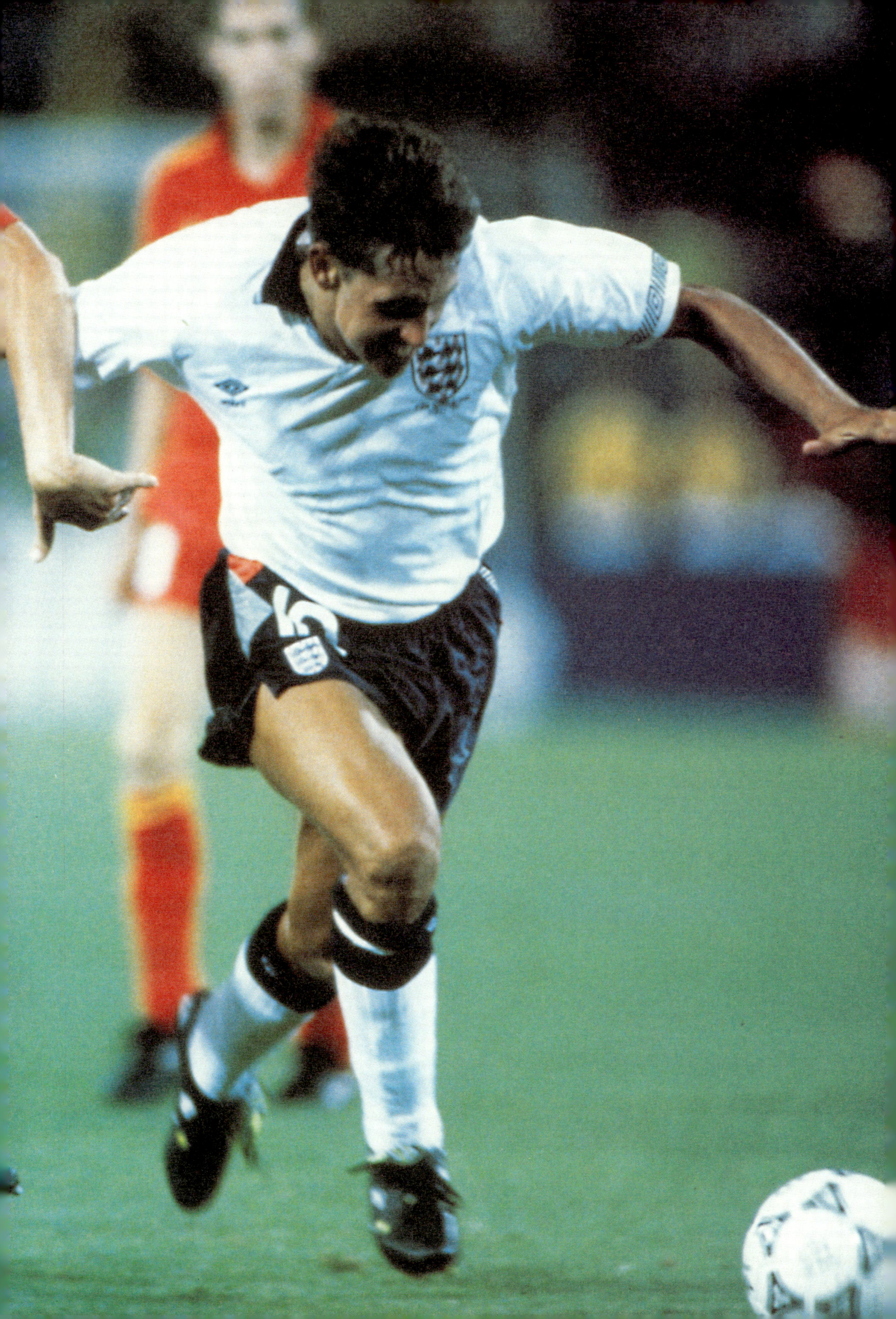

GARY LINEKER

During 1990-1, Lineker scored a total of 15 League goals and won an FA Cup-winners medal, when Spurs beat Nottingham Forest 2-1.

Lineker is undoubtedly England's greatest ambassador for the game and to his credit, he has never been booked or sent off throughout his career.

With 65 caps to his credit he was made England captain in the absence of the injured Bryan Robson, a role fitting to his level and great experience.

Lineker is also a talented cricketer and snooker player. A member of the MCC, he still plays cricket to the highest standard and could have been equally successful had he chosen to make it his career. Luckily for England and the game, he chose football and has become one of the truly great players in modern times.

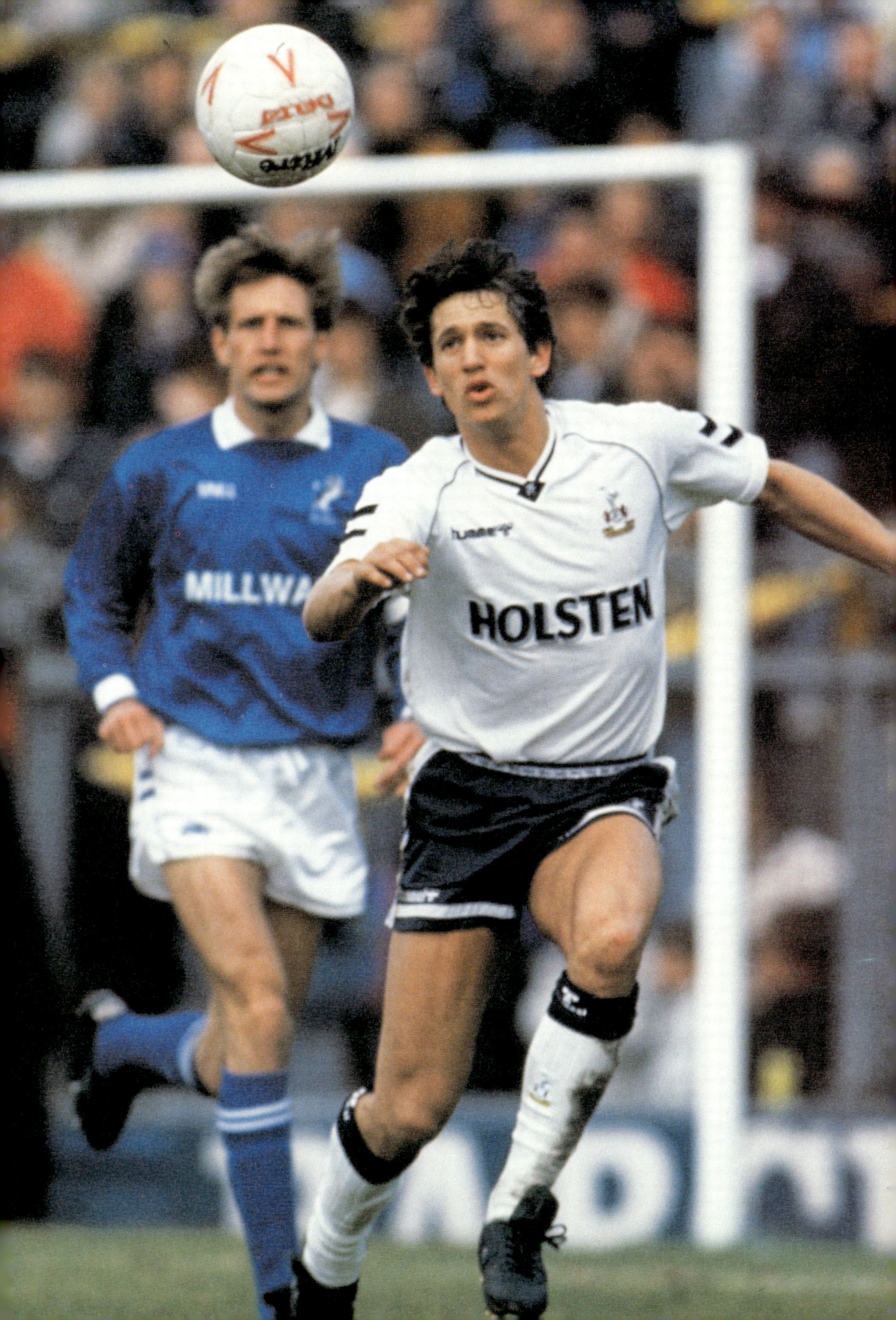
HOLSTEN
MILLWA

DEAN SAUNDERS

Welsh striker Dean Saunders was born on 21 June 1964, the son of a former Liverpool and Swansea Town player, Roy Saunders. Dean began his career with his home-town club, Swansea City (formerly Swansea Town) in 1982. He joined the club soon after their spectacular rise from the Fourth to the First Division. However, when he made his League debut in October 1983, against Charlton, City were heading for relegation.

Towards the end of the 1983-4 season, Saunders had established a regular first-team place, but despite his efforts, Swansea were relegated for the second successive season, this time to Division Three.

Although Saunders was City's top scorer, the following season he went on loan to Cardiff City and at the end of the season was given a free transfer to Brighton and Hove Albion.

In his first season at Brighton, he scored 19 goals and gained his first senior cap for Wales against the Republic of Ireland. It seemed his move to the south coast had finally changed his luck.

In 1987 Oxford United bought Saunders with a view to maintaining their place in the First Division. Their £600,000 investment brought the desired results, and Saunders scored two vital goals against Luton in the penultimate match of the season to ensure their First Division status. The following season, however, Oxford went down to Division Two, though Saunders remained United's top scorer. It was not long before he returned to top flight football when Derby County signed him for £1 million, after only ten appearances in the Second Division. A great deal of controversy surrounded the deal and Oxford manager, Mark Lawrenson, was sacked after a dispute with the board of directors.

At the Baseball Ground he scored 14 goals in his first full season.

During 1990-1, Saunders had scored a total of 21 goals, including 17 in the League, but despite his efforts Derby did not escape relegation to the Second Division. However, his performance and goal-getting skills were noted by several managers looking for a top class striker.

After some speculation that Saunders would join Everton, arch rivals Liverpool clinched a surprise late bid. A British record deal of £2.9 million, secured Dean to play alongside another ex Derby County star Mark Wright and also brought together the successful Welsh national side partnership of Saunders and Rush. Together with Barnes this makes a formidable forward line to help Liverpool maintain their position at the top of English football.

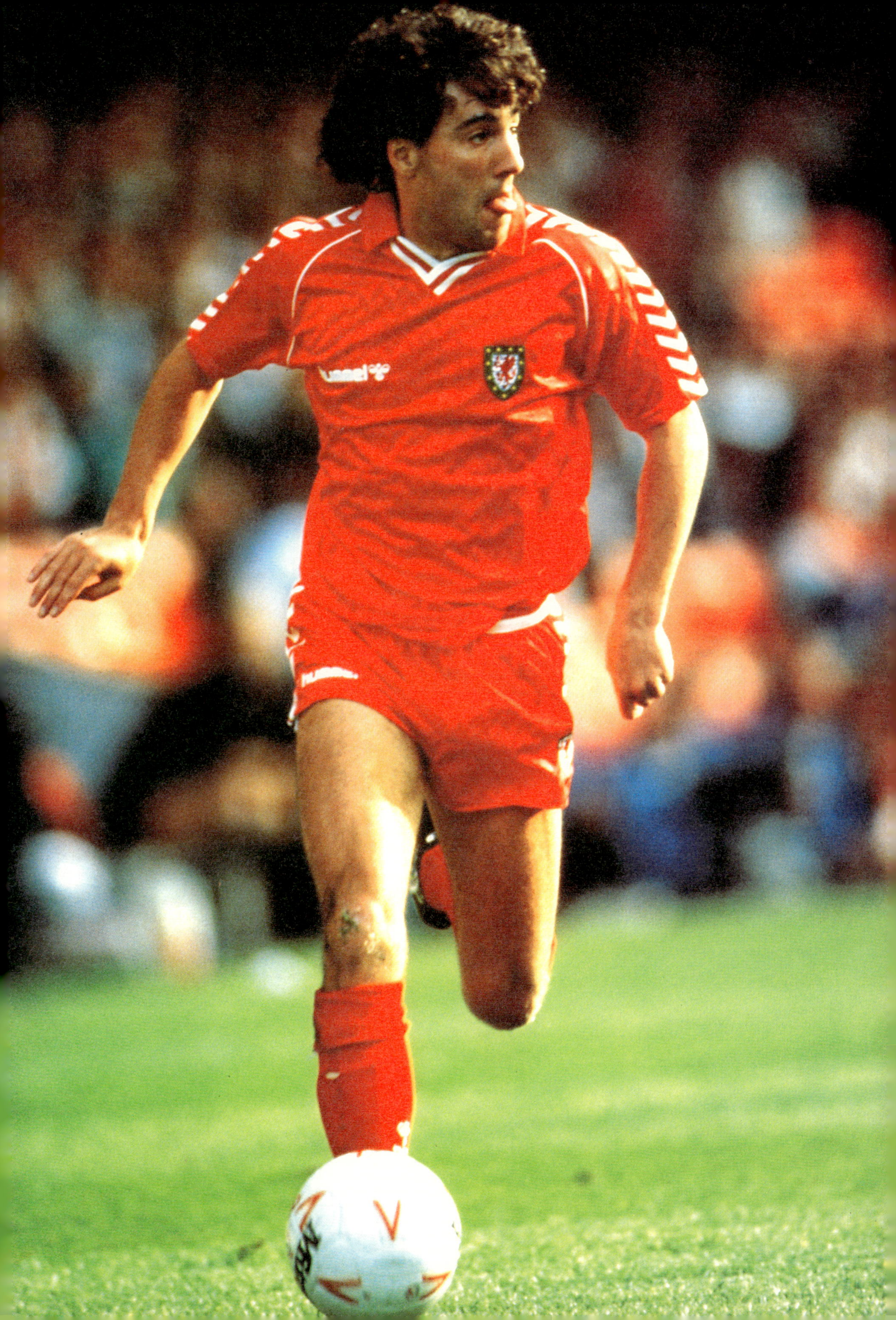

ALLY McCOIST

One of Scotland's top strikers, Ally McCoist was born in Bellhill, on 24 September 1962. He began with St. Johnstone, making his League debut on 7 April 1979 against Raith Rovers. He proved his flair for goal-getting at McDiarmid Park and in 1981-2 became the subject of the club's record transfer fee, when he moved to Sunderland for £400,000.

However, the move to Wearside was not successful and Ally could not reproduce his top form. After just two seasons he returned to Scotland with Rangers, in what was the best move of his career. He has since become a hero at Ibrox Park and his prolific goalscoring has helped Rangers to maintain their position at, or near, the top of the Premier Division.

During 1986-7, Ally scored a total of 33 goals in 44 appearances for Rangers, his personal best over any one season.

At the end of 1990-1 Rangers were Scottish Champions and Ally had scored a total of 18 goals, including 11 in the League, making him Rangers' joint top League scorer with Mo Johnston.

During his seven seasons at Ibrox, McCoist has thrilled the supporters with a total of 150 goals. He was a member of the Scottish World Cup team in Italy 1990, where he played in one match and was substitute in the other two. He has won 30 full caps for his country.

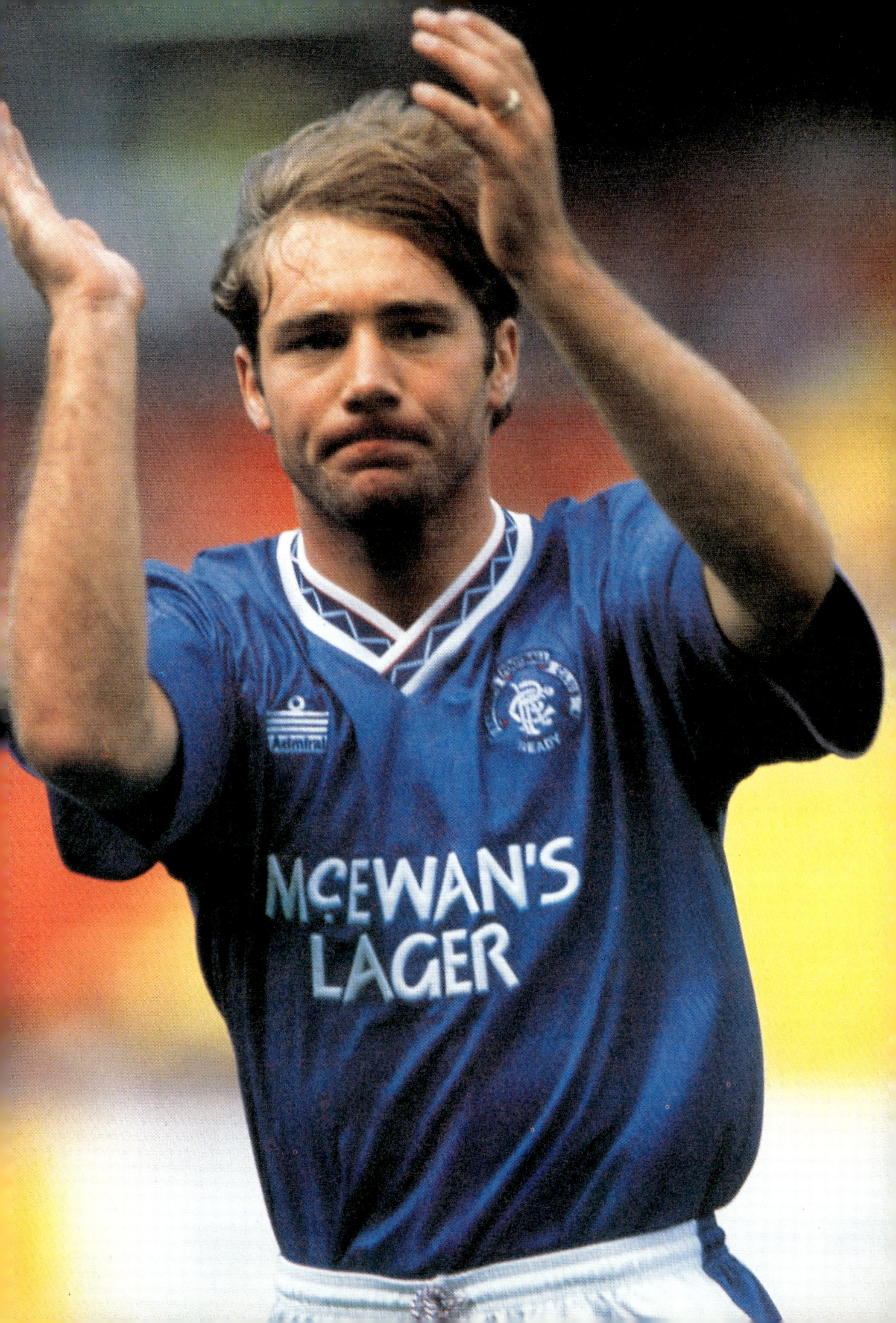
Admiral
McEWAN'S
LAGER

TEDDY SHERINGHAM

Teddy was born on 2 April 1966 at Highams Park. He began his career with Millwall during the 1983-4 season, after a period in the apprentice ranks. After a short time on loan to Aldershot during 1984-5, he returned to Millwall and steadily improved his goal tally. During 1987-8 he scored a total of 22 goals in 42 league appearances and Millwall won the Second Division Championship. After only two season in the First Division Millwall were relegated, but Teddy still reached a total of 17 league and cup goals. At the end of 1990-1 Teddy finished as the Football Leagues top scorer, with a remarkable 33 League goals and 38 in total. However Millwall just missed out on First Division football by losing to Brighton in the play offs. However, his performances in the 1990/91 season have been noted by several First Division managers looking to strengthen their strike force.

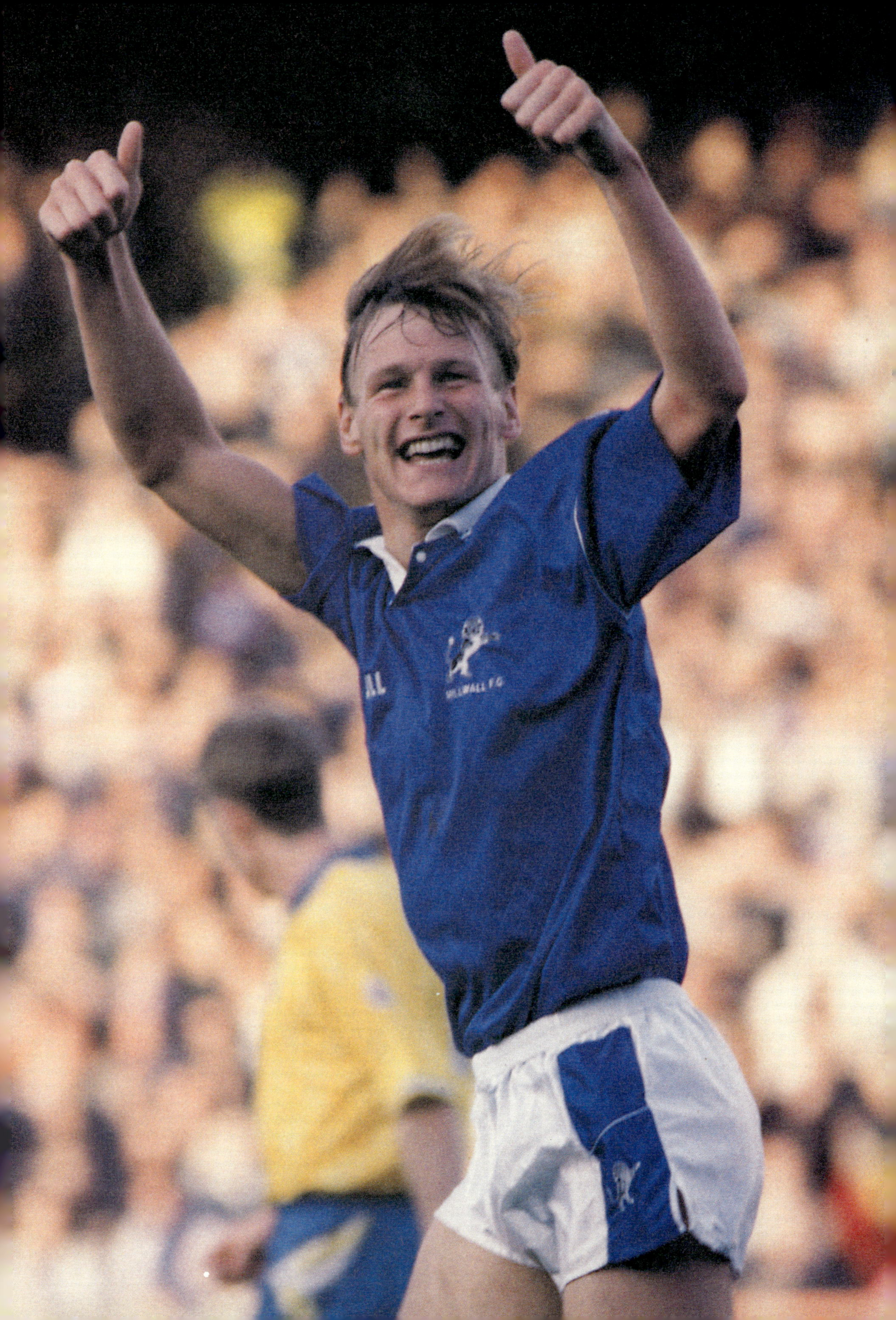

DAVID PLATT

Born at Chadderton, near Oldham, on 10 June 1966, Platt began playing as a junior with Manchester United, but was released in 1984 without ever playing in the first team.

He joined Crewe Alexandra in 1984 and made his League debut against Mansfield Town on 26 January 1985. He began in a midfield position, but nevertheless scored five goals during the season and kept his place in the first team without missing a match.

During the 1986-7 season, Platt scored a total of 23 goals in 43 appearances, making him the third highest scorer in the Fourth Division. He shattered the club record of 20 years standing by scoring more goals in one season than any other player.

In 1988, Dario Gradi, the manager at Crewe, who had a great influence on David's career, advised him to join Aston Villa, after the Second Division club, along with Watford and Hibernian, showed an interest in signing him. Platt, of course, took Gradi's advice and moved to Villa in a £200,000 transfer deal. The move proved to be successful for both the club and David and he found in Graham Taylor another manager who made a great contribution to his development.

Platt was a key player in the promotion race which Villa eventually clinched and they returned to the First Division at the end of 1987-8. In the penultimate match of the season David's goal in the 1-0 victory over Bradford City, who were also chasing the title, ultimately saw Villa into Division One.

The first season in the top flight was a great success for Platt. He scored seven League goals and six in the Littlewood's Cup. In the FA Cup, he scored one goal when Villa came from 2-0 down, to win 3-2, ironically against former club, Crewe. Villa have consolidated their success and remain a strong First Division team. In 1990, Platt was voted Player of the Year by his fellow professionals, and in the same year made his England debut against Italy. He scored three times in the 1990 World Cup and emerged as one of the stars of Bobby Robson's England squad.

In the 1990-1 season, Platt finished amongst the top five scorers in the First Division and had scored a total of 19 League goals and 24 in all competitions. Despite being pursued by Italian club, Bari, with a very lucrative financial package, Platt has pledged to remain at Villa for the forseeable future and the fans at Villa Park can look forward to more spectacular goals next season.

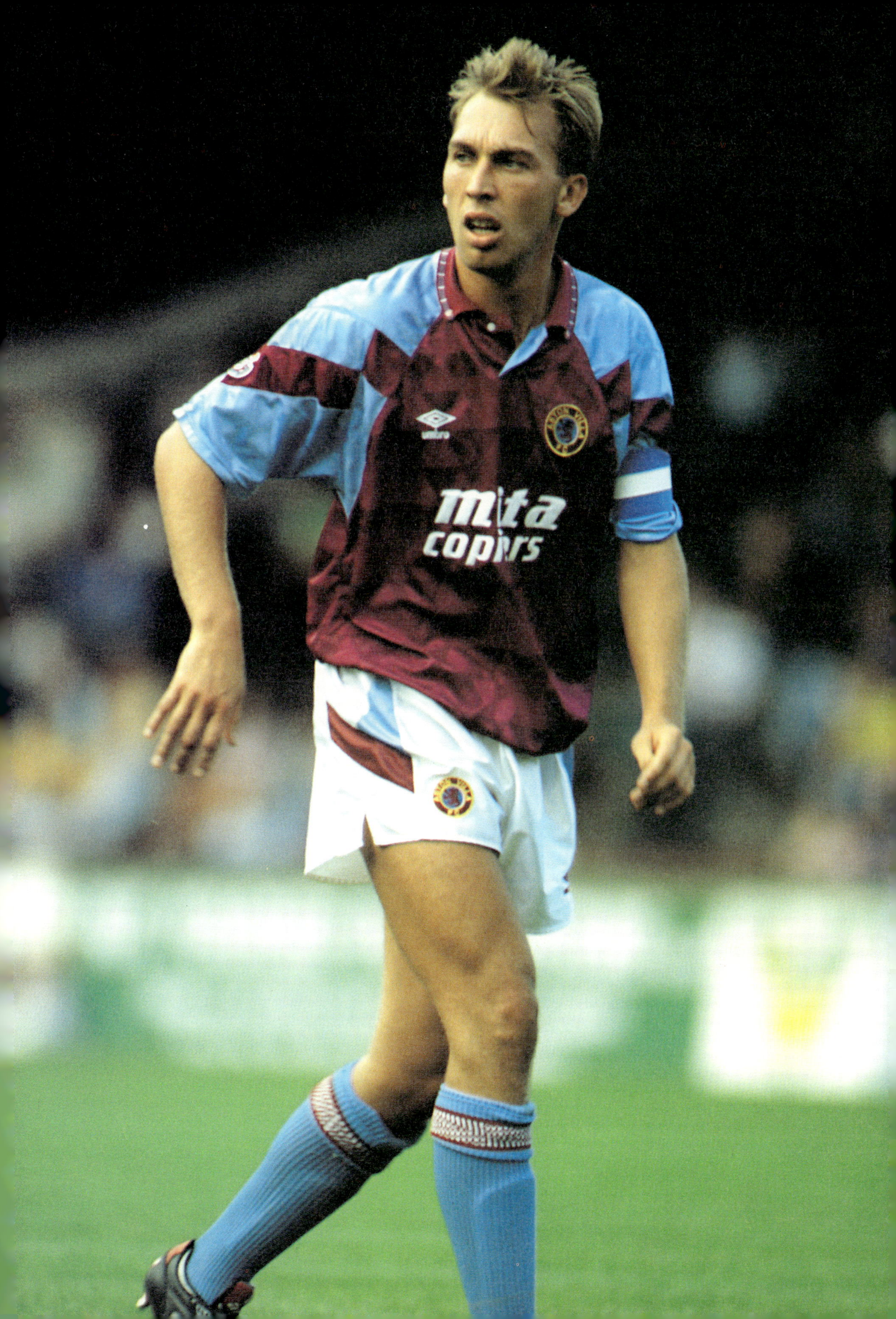
mita

NIGEL CLOUGH

Nigel was born in Sunderland on 19 March 1966, the son of one the most famous and respected figures in football, Brian Clough. Not surprising, he was football crazy as a youngster and has inherited much of his father's talent in the art of scoring goals.

Nigel grew up in Derby and began playing in the Derbyshire Sunday League. He was spotted by the Nottingham Forest coaching staff when he was playing semi-professional football with Heanor Town and joined Forest as an amateur. He was then invited to sign as a professional and made his League debut on 26 December 1984. Apart from the pressures all top flight footballers have to overcome, Nigel, of course, had to cope with the fact that his father was also the boss.

Clough soon proved his worth, demonstrating brilliant passing skills and a natural talent for scoring goals with deadly accuracy. During 1987-8, he scored 19 goals in 34 appearances and had already been selected for the England Under-21 side.

Nigel has so far remained a one-club player, despite Italian side, Pisa, making a bid for him during 1989-90. He has no plans to go abroad in the foreseeable future, and remains happy to pursue his career with Forest.

The 1990-1 season was a great success for Nigel. He had a good Cup-run, and was a key player in helping Forest to the Final. In a fourth round replay, he scored against Newcastle United, with Forest winning 3-1.

However, on the biggest day of his career, Forest were beaten in the FA Cup Final going down 2-1 after extra-time to Tottenham Hotspur. During the season, Clough scored a total of 20 goals, including 14 in the League.

Graham Taylor, the England manager, selected him to go on tour during the summer of 1991 and Nigel looks set for a successful international career.

An exceptionally gifted player, he is now established in his own right, no longer under the giant shadow of his father. He is always cool under pressure and often links up with Stuart Pearce to produce blistering goals. He has undoubtedly inherited his father's talent for the game. Nigel is modest by nature and does not relish being in the public eye.

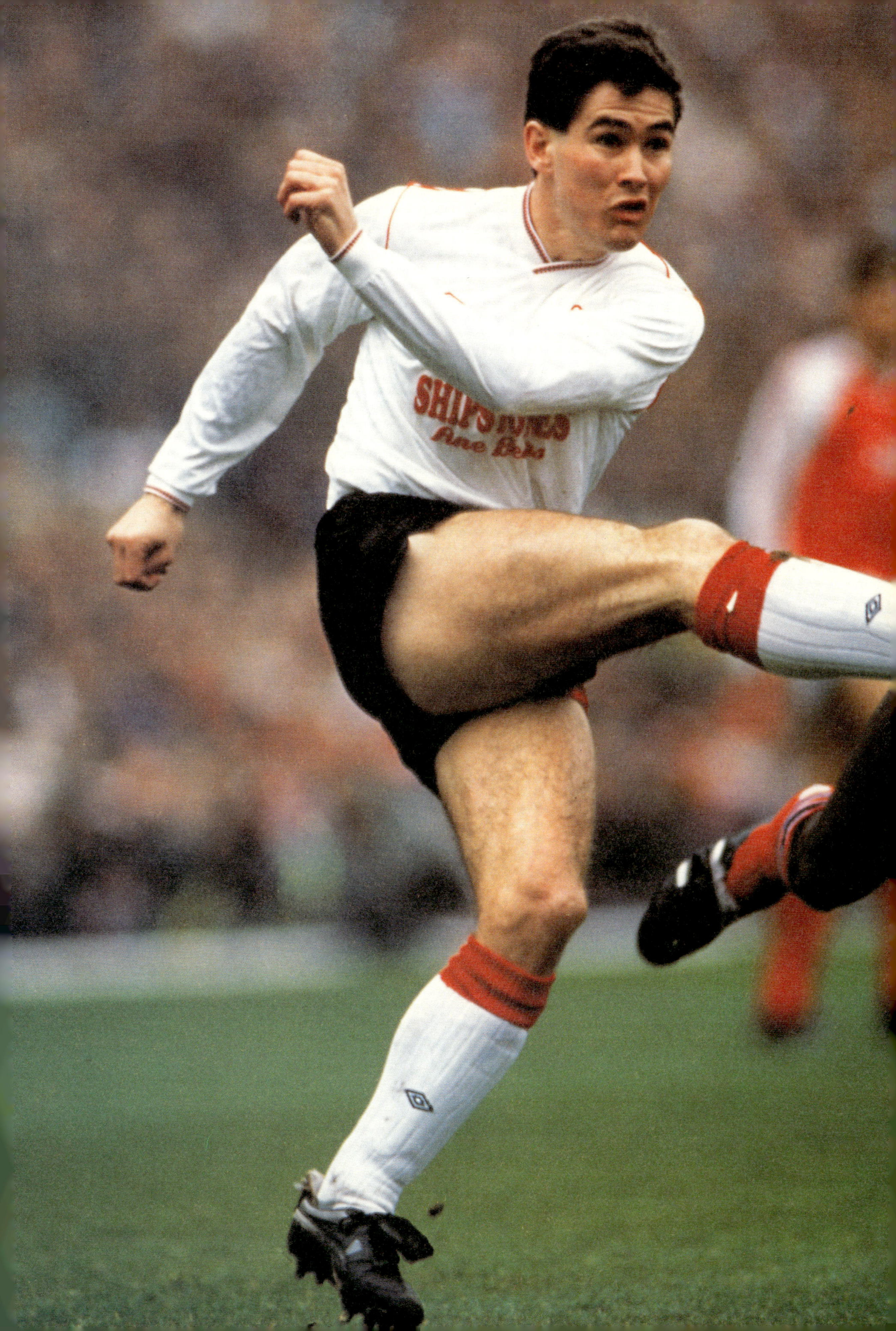
SHIPSTONES

IAN WRIGHT

During the 1990-1 season, Ian Wright proved he is amongst the finest strikers in the First Division and has been vital to Palace's success.

Born in Woolwich, London on 3 November 1963, Ian already holds the record as Palace's top all-time scorer in Divisions One and Two. By April 1991, he had notched up a total of 216 League appearances and scored 83 goals.

He began playing for Greenwich and came to Selhurst Park in 1985, where he soon gained a reputation as a prolific goalscorer. His partnership with Mark Bright is one of the most effective in the First Division and the pair are renowned for their exciting play and spectacular goals.

During the 1989-90 season Wright was Palace's leading goalscorer with 24 League goals in 42 appearances and a total of 33 goals in all.

Despite suffering two broken legs in 1990, he recovered to play for the England 'B' team and scored two goals in the FA Cup Final at Wembley against Manchester United, though Palace eventually lost 1-0 in the replay.

In 1990-1 Ian had an outstanding season and was amongst the top five leading goalscorers in the First Division, with a total of 15 League goals and 25 in all by May 11 1991. He had a tremendous game at Wimbledon on 4 May, when he scored a hat-trick in Palace's 3-0 victory. His second goal was a brilliant individual performance, resulting in a fine lob from 45 yards.

Wright made his debut for England in the same season, against Cameroon, and is widely tipped to become Gary Lineker's successor in the England team.

Wright, and Palace, look positioned for another great season in 1991-2, and Ian has proved, without doubt, he is worthy of a regular place in Graham Taylor's England side.

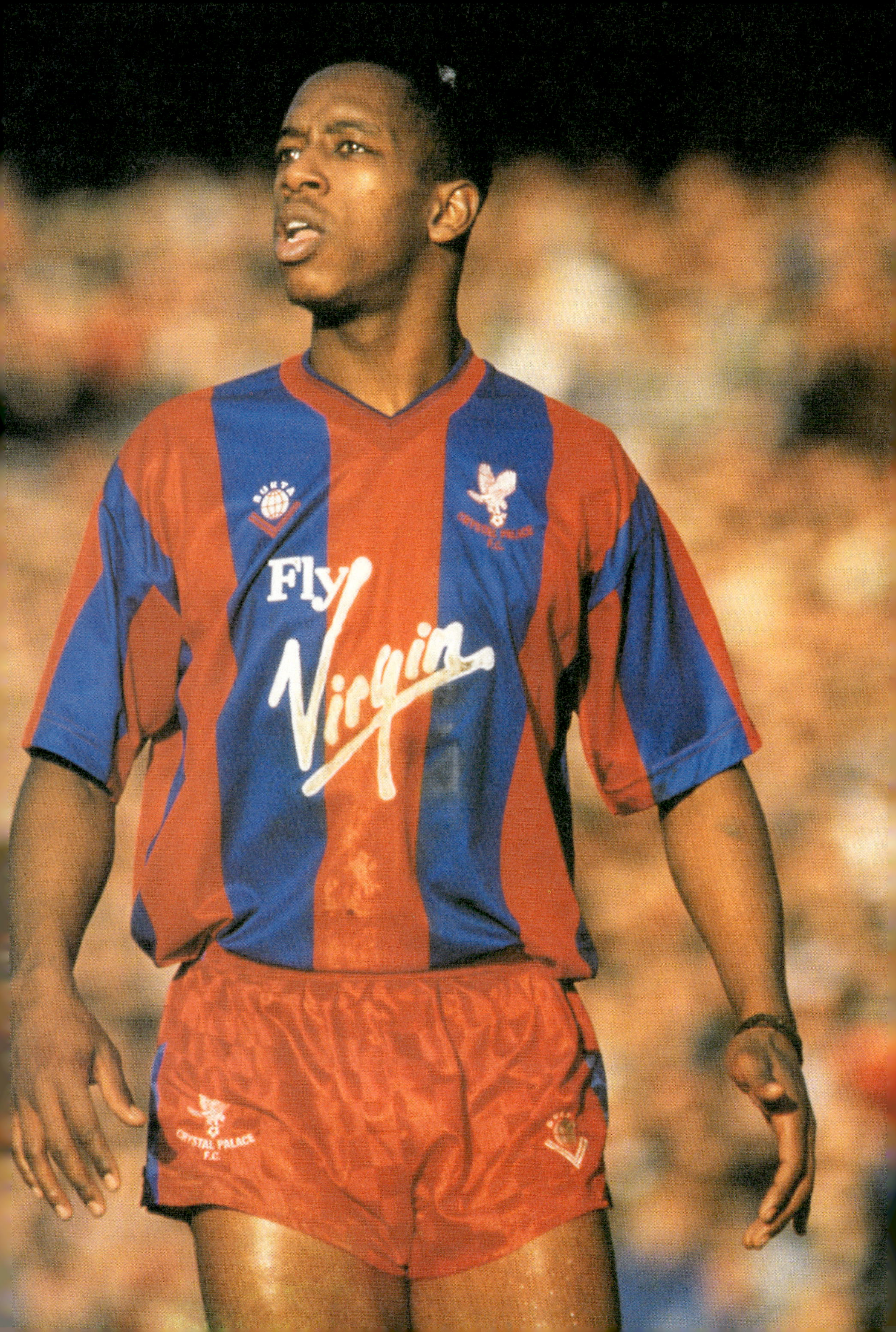
Fly
Virgin
CRYSTAL PALACE
F.C.

MO JOHNSTON

Mighty Mo's chequered career began with Partick Thistle in 1980, where, over four seasons, he proved his worth as a top goalscorer. He was born in Glasgow on 30 April 1963 and became one of Scotland's best known players during the 1980s.

He moved to Watford in 1983, but stayed for just over one season, before returning to Scotland with Celtic. Over three seasons he scored a total of 53 goals for the club, before being transferred to French club, Nantes, in June 1987 in a £1 million deal.

Graeme Souness brought Mo back to Scotland in a sensational deal, when he paid £1.5 million to Nantes, in the summer of 1989. Johnston snubbed his old club Celtic in favour of Rangers, in a very controversial transfer. At the time, Souness considered him to be the best striker in Europe and Mo justified his value by producing some brilliant football and netting many spectacular match-winning goals.

He has won nearly 40 full Scotland caps and, despite a stomach injury, played in all three matches in the 1990 World Cup, scoring one of Scotland's two goals. However, Scotland were disappointing in Italy and failed to qualify for the second round.

During 1990-1, Mighty Mo finished second highest scorer in the Premier Division with a total of 19 goals, including 11 League goals.

With the appointment of Graeme Souness as Liverpool manager towards the end of 1990-1, there is much speculation as to whether he will bring Mighty Mo south of the border. Certainly anything seems possible in the controversial career of the talented Scottish striker.

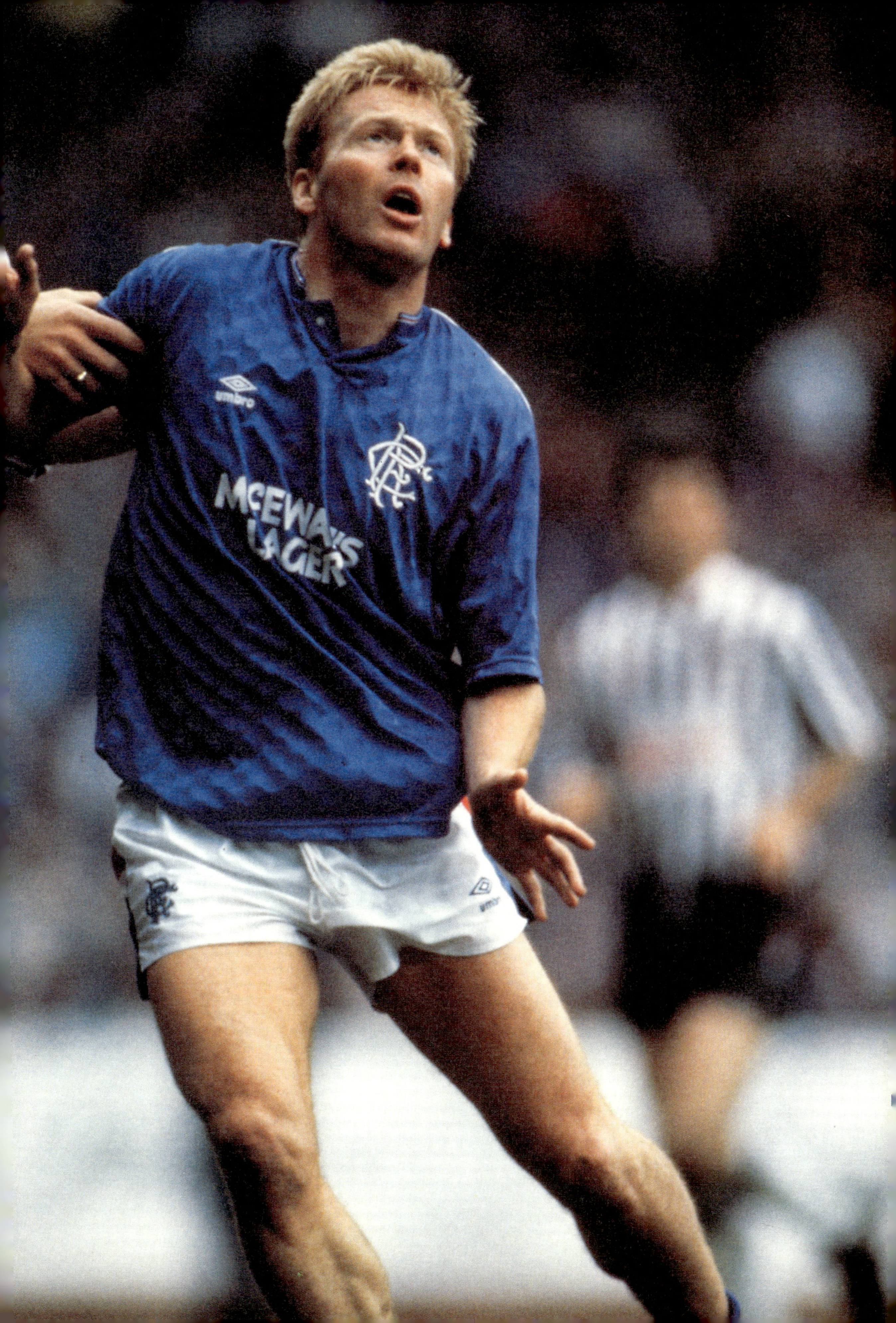
umbro
McEWAN'S
LAGER
umbro

ALAN SMITH

Gunner's striker Alan Smith was born in Birmingham on 21 November 1962 and began his career with Alvechurch. He was signed by Leicester City and made his League debut against Charlton Athletic, on 28 August 1982. He remained at Leicester for five seasons and scored 73 League goals for the club in 191 appearances.

He moved to Highbury in May 1987 for a fee of £850,000 and made his debut against Liverpool on 15 August. He soon gained a regular place in George Graham's team and the following season he was the top scorer in the First Division with 23 League goals and the winner of a League Championship medal. He was also voted the Arsenal Supporters' Club Player of the Year 1988-9 season.

He had another terrific season in 1990-1, when he equalled his 1988-9 achievement and was the leading scorer in the First Division, winning the Adidas 'Golden Boot' with a total of 22 League goals as well as helping Arsenal to another League Championship title. However, in the FA Cup, Smith's goal against Spurs in the semi-final was not enough to give Arsenal victory and they went down 3-1.

Smith has won England 'B' honours and five full caps for his country. At 6ft 3in, he is a superb header of the ball and finds the net with precision and accuracy. He can create openings and finish in spectacular style with his lethal right foot. He is particularly dangerous in the box and his lightning reflexes often produce goals.

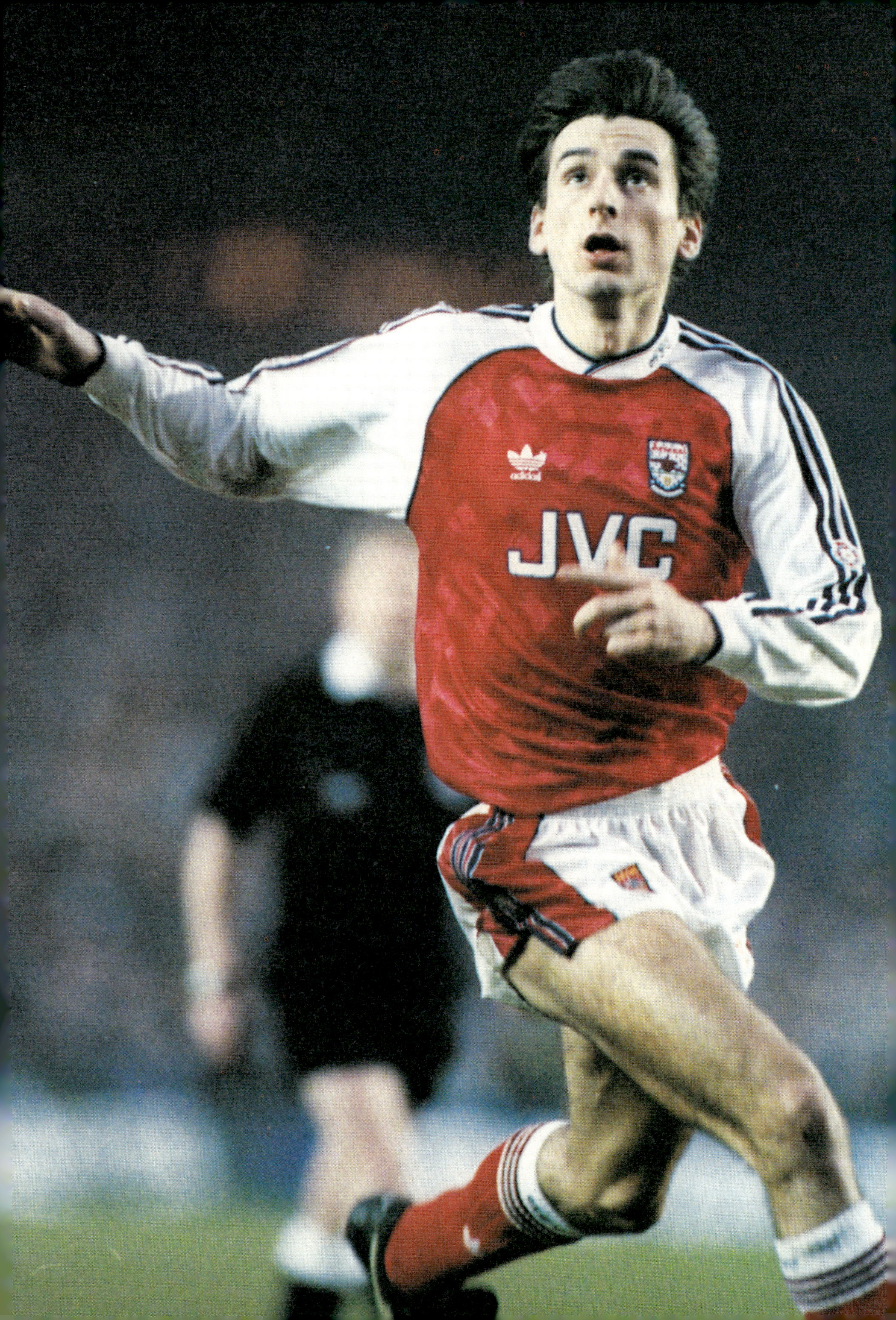
JVC

NIALL QUINN

The 6ft 4in Irishman was born in Dublin on 6 October 1966 and made his League debut for Arsenal against Liverpool in December 1985. He joined Arsenal during the 1983-4 season, but it was not until 1985-6 that he gained a first team place.

He remained at Arsenal until 1989-90, but during his last three seasons at Highbury made only 20 League appearances due to the dominance of striker Alan Smith. However, he made an instant impact on his move to Manchester City in March 1990 in an £800,000 deal and finally found the success and first-team place that eluded him. He scored in his debut match for City against Chelsea in a 1-1 draw and went on to score some crucial goals for the club.

He was a member of Jack Charlton's Republic of Ireland World Cup squad and scored the equalising goal against Holland which ensured Ireland's place in the second round of the tournament.

Quinn had a tremendous 1990-1 season and hit peak form with City. He scored 20 League goals during the season, finishing third highest scorer behind Smith and Chapman. In total, he scored 22 goals in all competitions. He was also voted Manchester City's Player of the Year after his personal best season.

Niall is firmly committed to City and has signed a contract which will keep him at Maine Road until 1995, where he hopes to be winning honours in the near future. The 'gentle giant' of soccer is undoubtedly one of the most accurate target men in the game today.

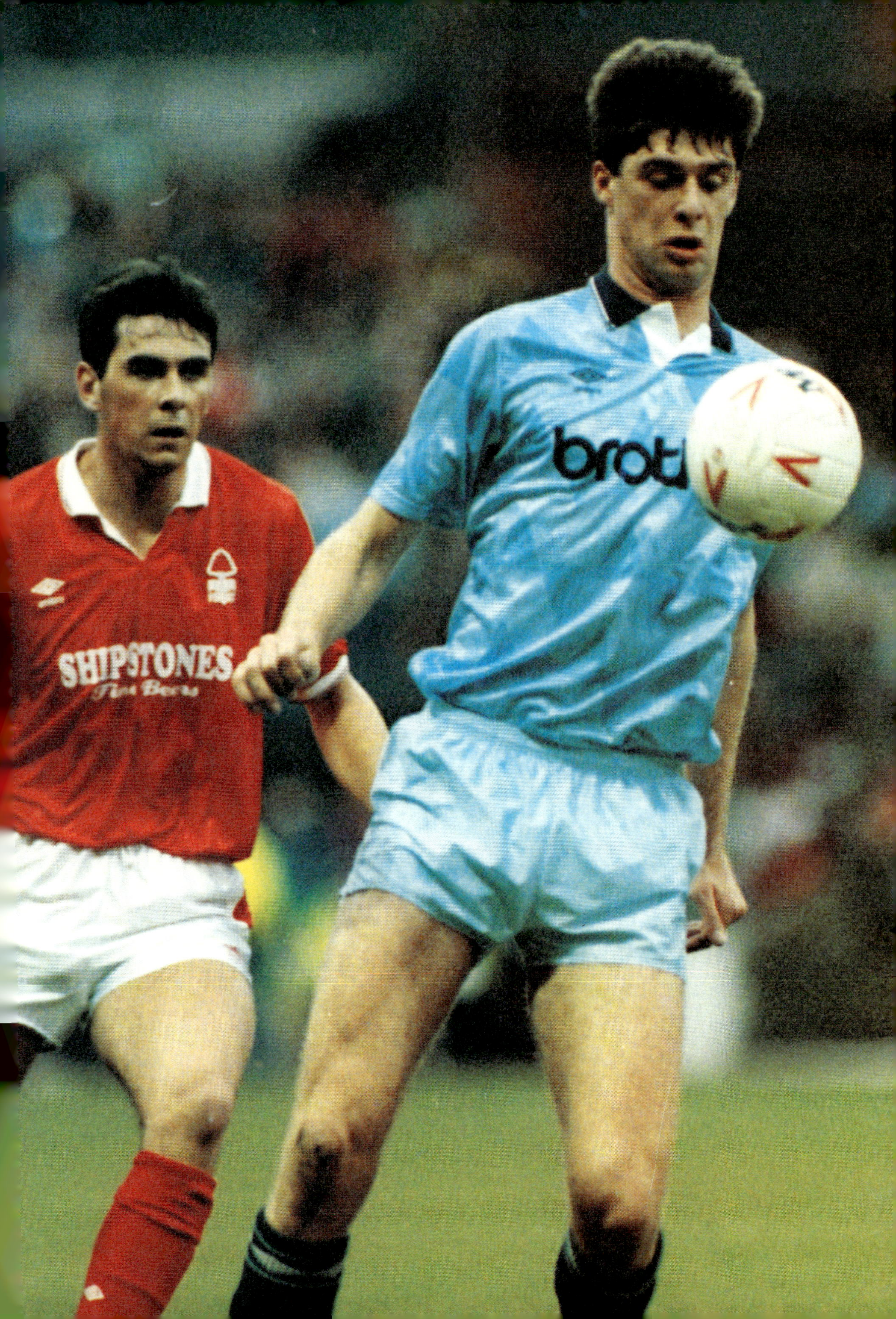
SHIPSTONES
brot

PETER BEARDSLEY

Peter began playing with local team, Wallsend Boys Club. Since then his career has progressed to take him to the mighty Liverpool. His professional debut was with Carlisle United in August 1979, when his transfer fee was a new set of shirts for the Wallsend team! However, in 1987 he commanded a fee of £1,900,000, when Liverpool bought him from Newcastle United.

Beardsley was born in Newcastle-upon-Tyne in January 1961, and after unsuccessful trials with Gillingham, Oxford, Burnley and Cambridge United, he was taken on by Carlisle United.

After playing 102 games for Carlisle over three seasons, the club were forced to sell Beardsley to Vancouver Whitecaps. The following season, Ron Atkinson invited him to Manchester United for a trial period and Beardsley looked set to make his breakthrough in the English First Division. Sadly, it did not happen and he only made one appearance for United in the Football League Cup against Bournemouth and even then did not play the full 90 minutes. Beardsley returned to Vancouver, but in 1983 moved back to English soccer, fittingly to his home-town club, Newcastle United. At last, this was the move Beardsley had needed to change his career.

Success came quickly at St. James' Park. In his first season he scored 20 goals in 35 games and, together with Kevin Keegan and Chris Waddle, made up one of the finest forward lines ever seen at United. The Magpies gained promotion to the First Division at the end of the 1983-4 season and Beardsley maintained his prolific goalscoring, earning international recognition.

In January 1986, he made his debut for England when they won 4-0 against Egypt in the build-up to the World Cup, securing his place in the England squad for the finals in Mexico.

The following season, back at Newcastle, Beardsley was plagued by a series of injuries and he scored only five goals in 32 League games. Despite his disappointing season, Liverpool had been following him closely and his talent and reputation resulted in his departure to Merseyside for a record fee of £1.9 million in 1987.

In his first season at Anfield, Liverpool became League Champions and he was part of the FA Cup-winning side of 1989 when Liverpool won 3-2 against Everton after extra-time. Liverpool were again Champions in 1989-90, and Beardsley scored ten goals in 29 appearances.

With three brilliant seasons at Anfield behind him, Peter went to Italy in the World Cup 1990 and played in five matches, including two as a substitute, but unfortunately did not score.

At the close of the 1990-1 season, Liverpool finished second in the League to Arsenal, though Beardsley did not hold a regular first team place from mid-season onwards.

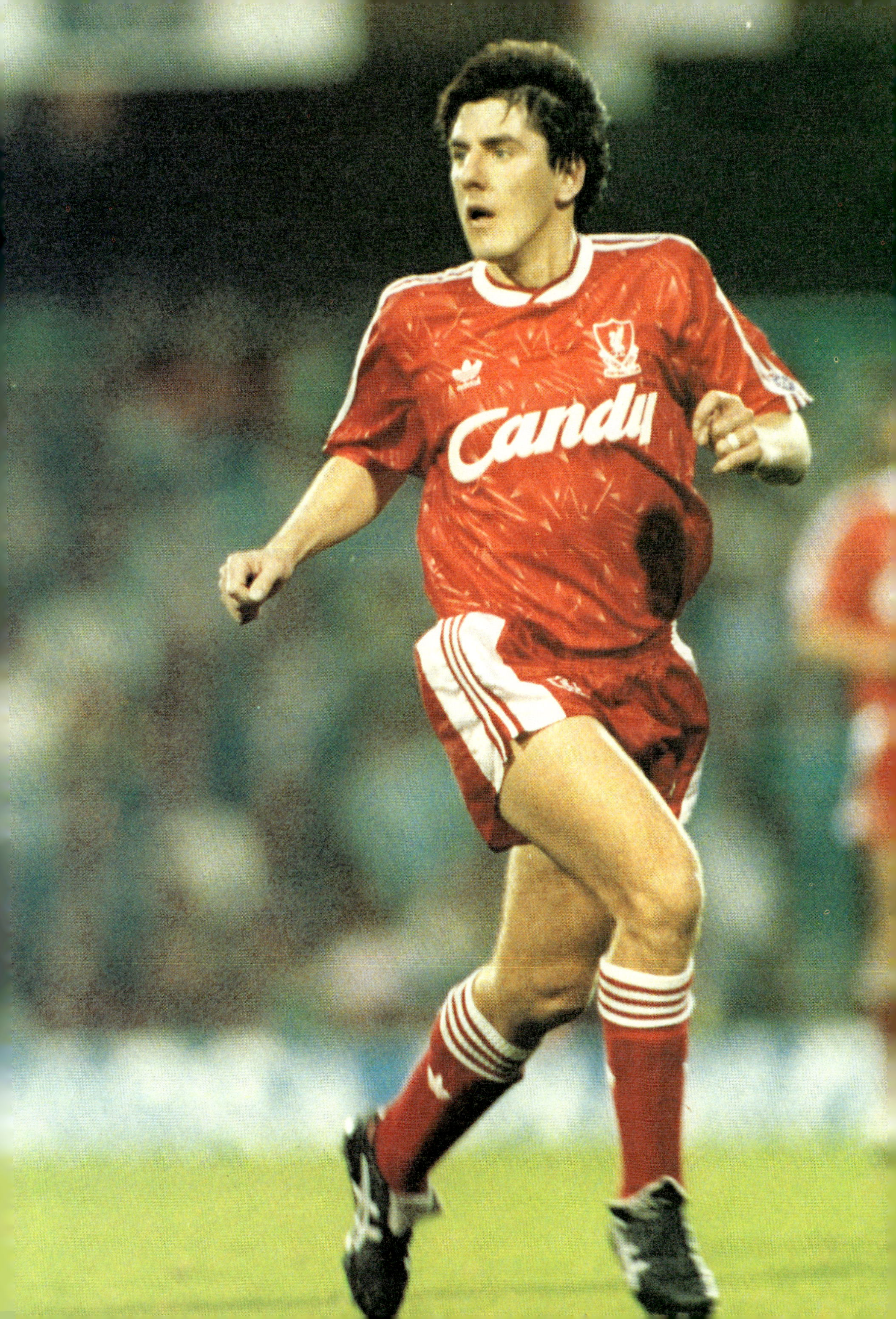
Candy

JOHN BARNES

John was born in Kingston, Jamaica on 7 November 1963, where his father was the skipper, and later the coach, of the Jamaican national team. The Barnes family came to England in 1976, and it was soon obvious John had inherited his father's talent and love of the game.

He was quickly snapped up by Fourth Division Watford in July 1981, after being spotted playing for Middlesex side, Sudbury Court. Two months later he made his first team debut against Oldham Athletic.

Watford's spectacular rise from the Fourth to the First Division was an incredible achievement and the following season they were runners-up in the League Championship to Liverpool. Barnes undoubtedly played a major part in Watford's meteoric rise and subsequent title challenge and, together with Luther Blissett, formed a formidable goalscoring duo. In 1984, Watford reached the FA Cup Final for the first time in their history but went down to a strong Everton side, losing 2-0. Barnes scored 65 goals in 233 League games for Watford during seasons 1981 to 1987.

In July 1987, a £900,000 transfer secured Barnes' move to Liverpool and on 15 August he made his debut in the famous red shirt in a 2-1 win at Arsenal. When he signed for Liverpool he had already won 30 England caps. It was the beginning of a new era at Liverpool with Barnes and Peter Beardsley, the two newcomers in the re-styled team.

Barnes soon became a favourite of the Anfield crowd and his good all-round game and blistering runs down the left wing, which often produced an accurate cross to Rush or Beardsley, soon brought results. Although predominantly left-footed, John can dribble his way past defenders on either side and his powerful shooting resulted in spectacular goals.

Liverpool became League Champions in Barnes' first season at Anfield, and he gave the team a new dimension with his magical skills. He had such a tremendous impact that he was voted Player of the Year by both the Football Writers and his fellow professionals in 1988.

The following season he was a member of the FA Cup-winning side when Liverpool beat local rivals Everton 3-2 after extra-time in 1989.

John can often produce a streak of unexpected brilliance that is sheer magic to watch and has great charisma and presence on the pitch. During the 1989-90 season he scored a total of 22 League goal in 34 appearances and his consistently outstanding form again earned him the FWA Footballer of the Year Award in 1990.

Barnes regularly plays for England but has never matched his Liverpool form in international football. In the 1990 World Cup, John won 5 England caps, but failed to score a goal.

In 1990-1, Barnes had scored a total of 16 League goals by May 11 and Liverpool finished runners-up in the League to Arsenal.

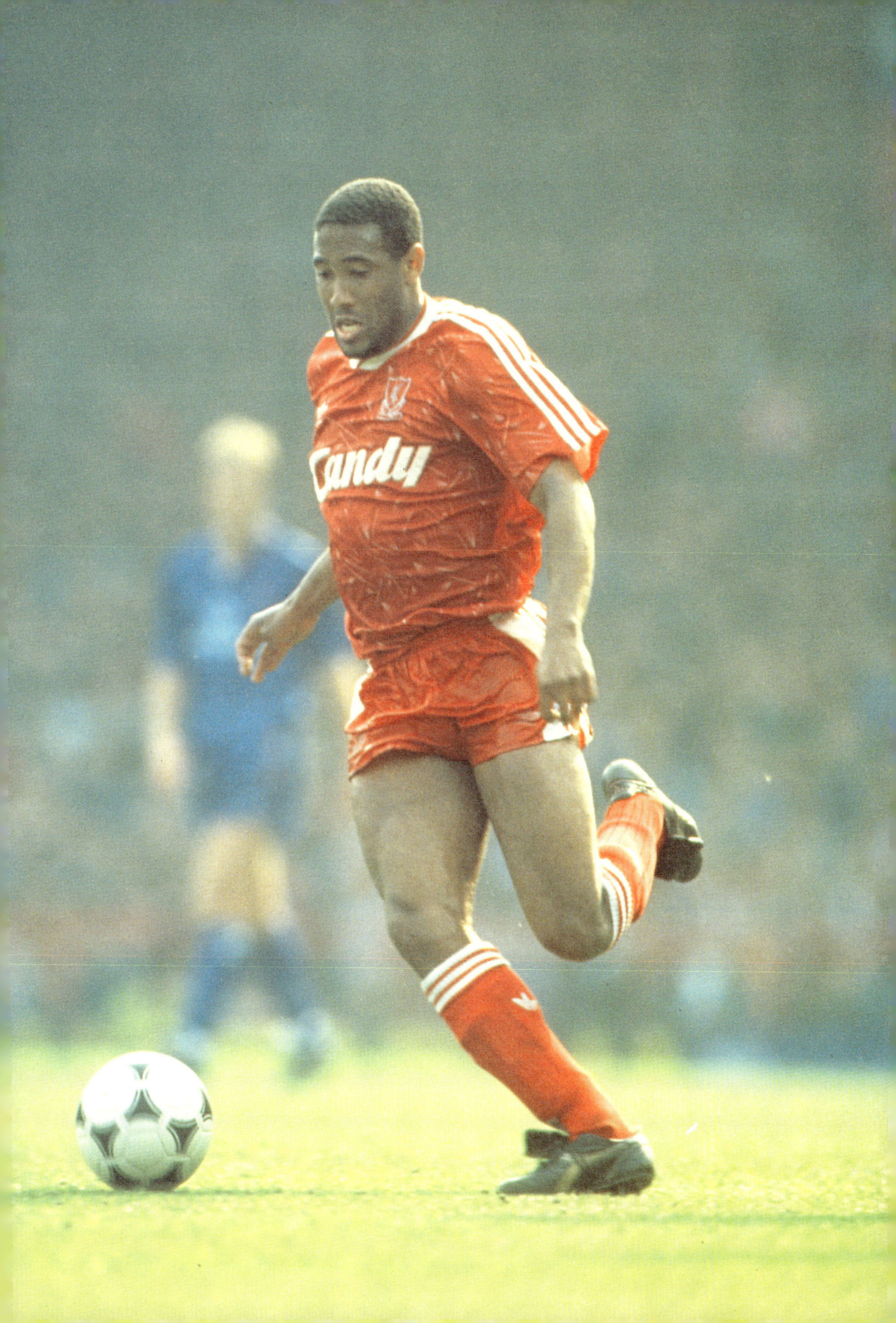
Candy

TONY COTTEE

Before he became a professional footballer with West Ham, Tony Cottee was a keen supporter of the Hammers, where he watched his idol, Bryan "Pop" Robson, from the terraces of his home-town club. He was born on 11 July 1965, joined the first team in the 1982-3 season through the apprentice ranks and remained for five seasons.

His career got off to a tremendous start and he soon proved his ability to score plenty of goals. His best season with the Hammers was in 1986-7 when he scored 22 League goals in 42 appearances. During his five years as a senior player with the club he scored 117 goals in 256 matches. He also won England youth and under 21 honours and made several substitute appearances for the full England team under Bobby Robson.

His move to Everton in the Summer of 1988 for £2 million brought a new challenge. In his debut for the Blues, against Newcastle United, Cottee got off to a flying start, scoring a hat trick.

In May 1989, he kicked off his first match for England against Scotland at Hampden, and has since gone on to win seven full caps.

Despite problems with form and fitness during 1990-1, he finished up amongst the leading goalscorers in the First Division and had netted a total of 24 goals at the end of the season.

Cottee's ambition is to score over 200 League goals and 300 altogether in his career. So far he has a total of 162 goals to his credit and the Everton fans can look forward to many more next season from this talented striker.

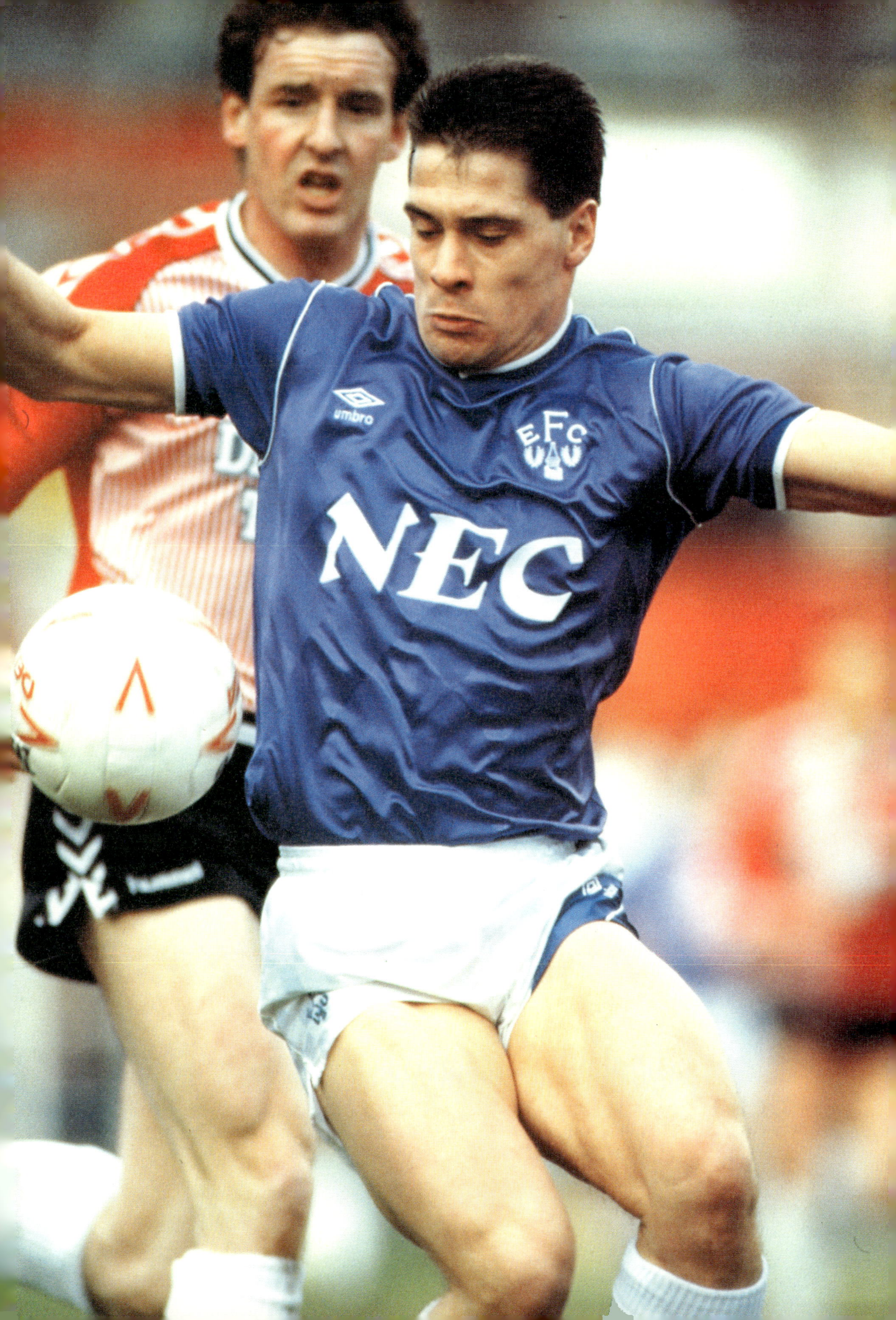
umbro
NEC

STEVE BULL

Steve Bull has been instrumental in Wolves' rise from the Fourth to the Second Division with his prolific goalscoring and deadly accurate shot.

Steve was born in the West Midlands, at Tipton on 28 March 1965. In the last 21 games of the 1986 season, Bull netted 12 goals. Unfortunately, Wolves just missed promotion and began the 1987-8 season still in Division Four. Bull scored a remarkable 34 League goals in 44 appearances in that season and Wolves took the title and promotion. In all, he scored a total of 52 goals, breaking the club record.

In the Third Division, Bull improved on his total and scored 37 League goals as Wolves took the Division Three Championship. Bull rapidly gained star status and his abundant goalscoring caught the attention of England manager, Bobby Robson. Having already won England Under-21 and England 'B' honours, Bull's brilliant striking power was rewarded with a full England debut against Scotland in 1989, where he came on as substitute and scored a terrific goal, his 55th of the season.

He began the 1989-90 season in Division Two and continued to find the back of the net with a total of 24 League goals. He was a member of the England World Cup squad in 1990 and played in four matches, three of these as a substitute, although failing to score.

During 1990-1, he finished second highest scorer in the Second Division with a total of 26 League goals. Many of the top First Division clubs have shown an interest in Bull, but he remains loyal to Wolves and has no desire to leave his Midlands roots. If Wolves are to return to their rightful place in the First Division, Steve Bull is just the man to help put them back in top flight football.

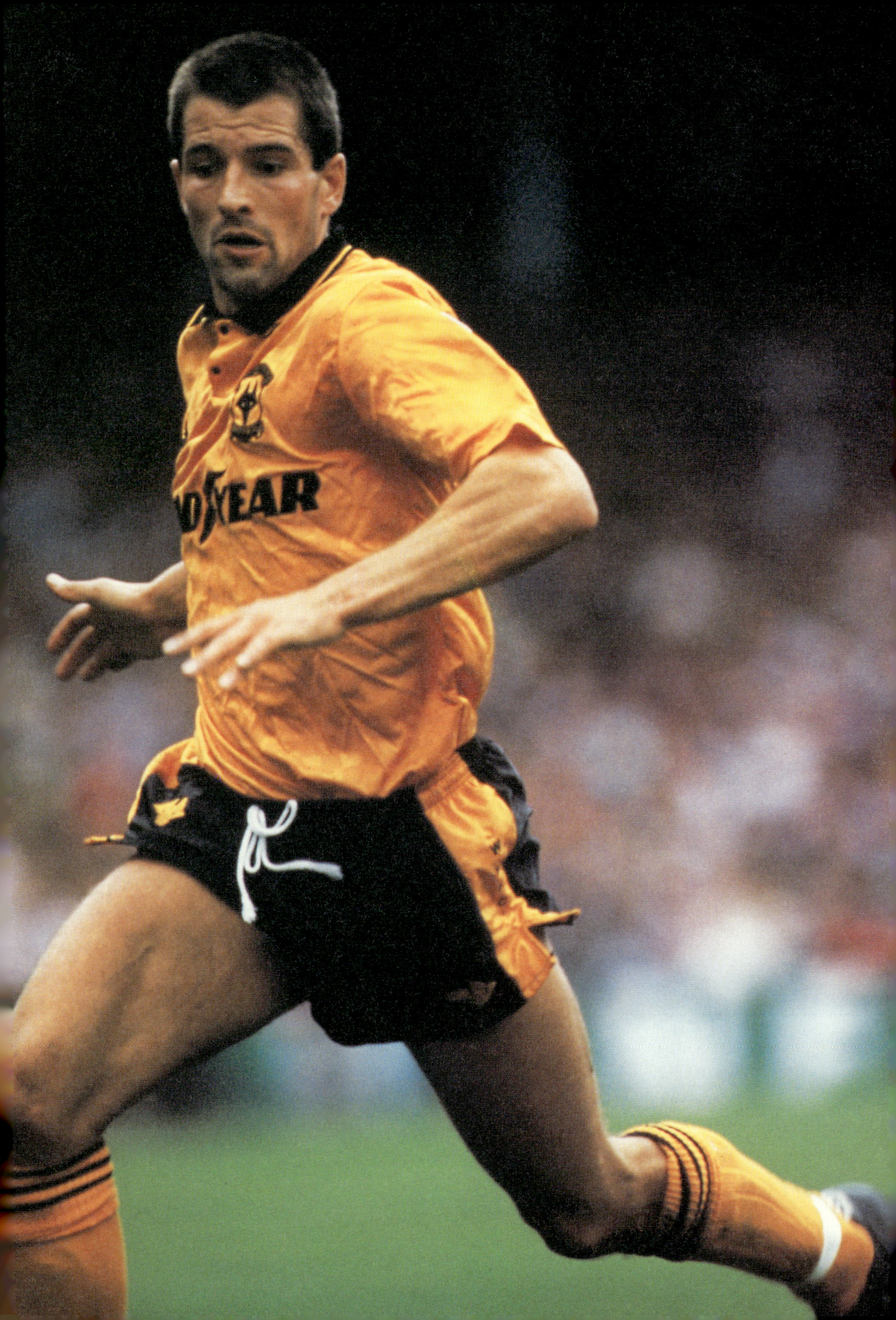

PAUL GASCOIGNE

After a brilliant World Cup in Italy, Paul Gascoigne became one of the most famous players in the game today. "Gazza-mania" swept the country and Paul's dazzling skills helped put England in the top four of international soccer.

Paul was born on 27 May 1967 in Gateshead. At school, he excelled in one subject, sport, and at the age of 14 he joined Newcastle as an apprentice. He made his first-team debut as a 17 year old on 13 April 1985, against QPR.

The following season he had established a permanent place in the team and scored nine goals, making him the second highest scorer behind Peter Beardsley. During 1986-7, he made 24 appearances for United, losing his place in the first half of the season to Paul Goddard. However before the season was over, Gazza was back for Newcastle and was a member of the England Under-21 team, competing in the UEFA tournament in Toulon.

During his time at Newcastle, he was nicknamed the "Mars Bar Kid" when the fans discovered his love of them. Paul has often had to fight the bulge and curb his love of junk food and chocolate bars. After another season at Newcastle, Gascoigne left his native north-east and made the move to Tottenham Hotspur in a £2,000,000 deal, where he teamed up with ex-Newcastle player, Chris Waddle.

He made his England debut when he came on as substitute against Denmark on 14 September 1988 and has since gone on to feature regularly in the England squad. He was voted the PFA's Young Player of the Year in 1988, the climax of a brilliant year in his career.

At Spurs, Gascoigne played a huge part in the team's revival, together with Waddle, Stewart and Walsh. In 1989, Terry Venables added Gary Lineker to his star line-up and Spurs' success was assured. Paul scored 6 goals in 34 appearances during the 1989-90 season when Spurs finished third.

In the 1990 World Cup, Gazza played in six matches. He endeared himself to the nation when he wept during the semi-final against West Germany after his second booking, which meant he would not play in the Final, had England qualified.

Spurs and Gazza had an outstanding 1990-1 season, finishing in the top half of the First Division and winning the FA Cup. Despite undergoing surgery a month earlier, Gazza played in the Cup semi-final at Wembley against Arsenal and scored the first of Spurs three goals in their 3-1 victory. Sadly, however, he did not share the glory in Spurs Cup Final win over Nottingham Forest, as he was stretchered off with a knee injury in the opening 15 minutes.

Towards the end of 1990-1 there had been great speculation as to whether Gazza would move to Italian club, Lazio. Despite his continued success with Spurs and advice from his fellow professionals to stay at White Hart Lane, he may make the move to Italy next season.

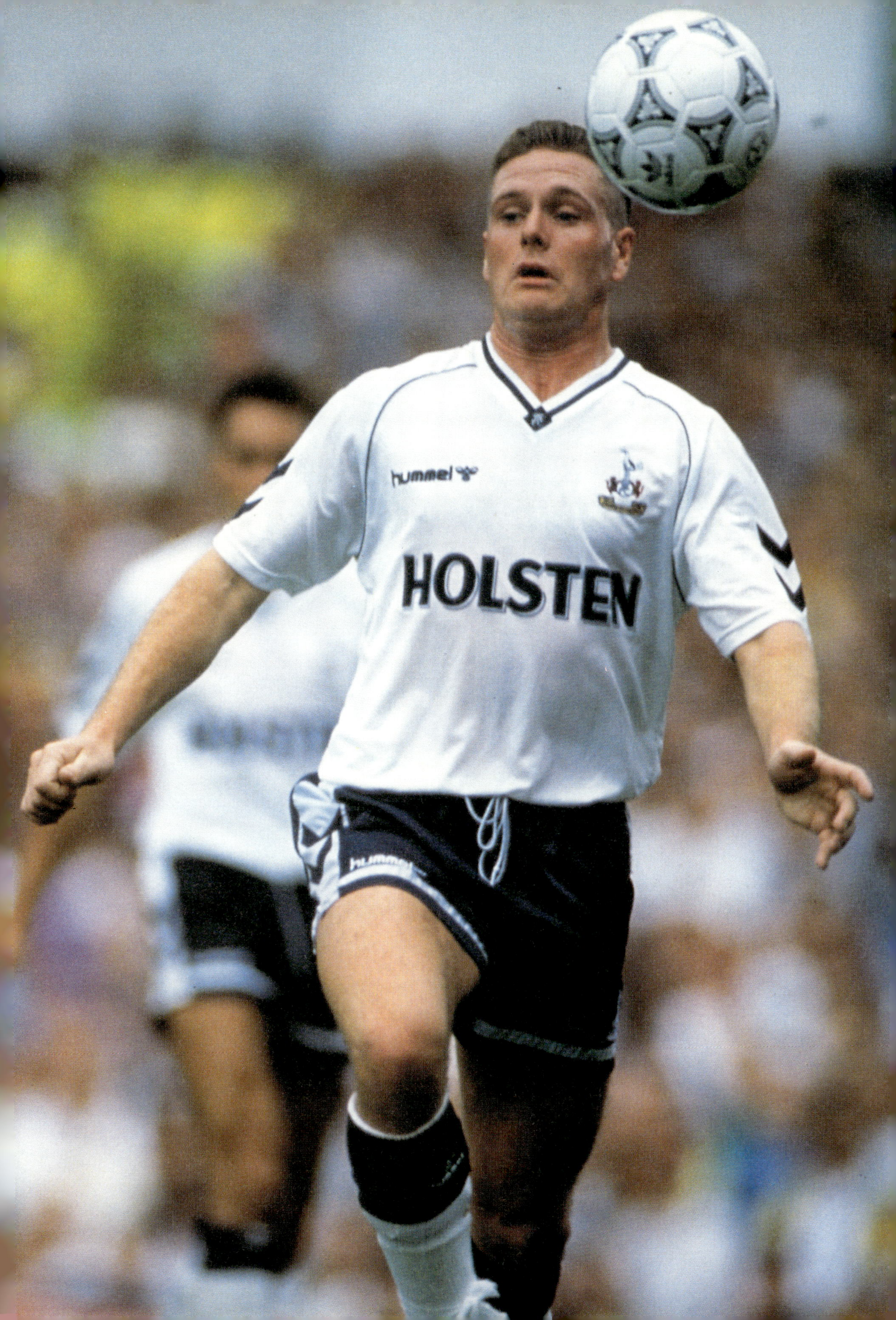
hummel
HOLSTEN
hummel

BRIAN DEANE

Brian Deane hails from Leeds and was born on 7 February 1968. He joined Doncaster Rovers as an apprentice and made his first team League debut against Swansea on 4 February 1986.

After three seasons with Doncaster, he was signed by Sheffield United for £30,000 in 1988. In his first season with United, he finished joint top scorer with a total of 30 goals, including 22 in the League. In 1989-90 he scored a total of 21 goals.

During 1990-1, Deane scored a total of 17 goals in all, though the Blades had a disappointing season.

Deane is especially powerful in the air, and at 6ft 3in his height has enabled him to net some spectacular headers. His natural talent has attracted the attention of England manager, Graham Taylor, and Deane was called up for the tour of Australia and New Zealand during June 1991. He won his first full cap during the match against New Zealand on 8 June.

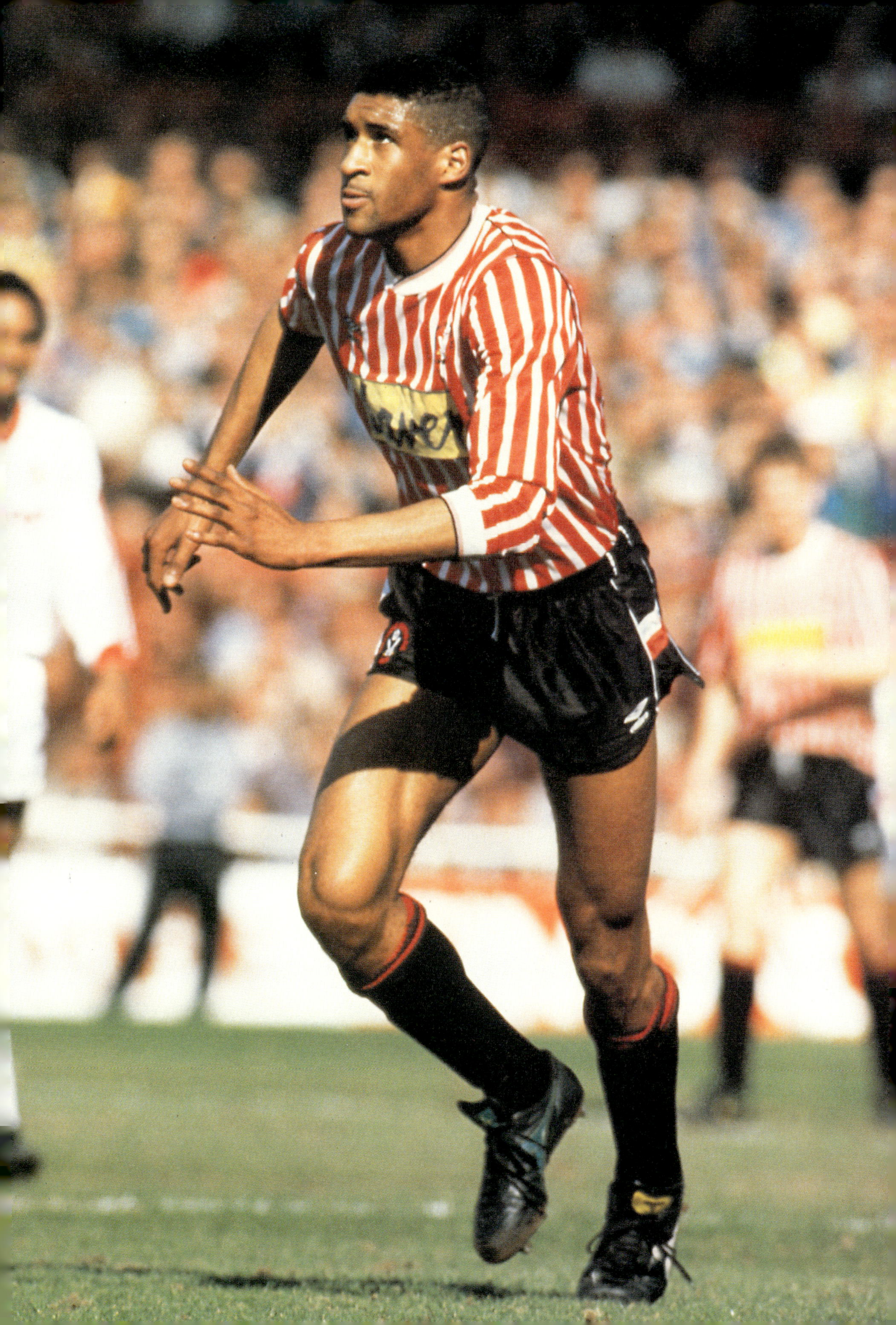

KERRY DIXON

Kerry Dixon was born on 24 July 1961, in Oak Road, Luton, right next to the Kenilworth Road ground, where his father was a professional footballer. Kerry began his career with Reading, after a brief period with Tottenham Hotspur as an apprentice and with Dunstable in the Southern League. He made his League debut for Reading against Walsall in August 1980, and over three seasons at Elm Park scored 51 goals.

His abundant goalscoring attracted the attention of Chelsea and in August 1983 he was signed for £175,000. During 1983-4, his first season with the Blues, he scored 28 League goals and 34 in all for the first team, giving him the highest individual total since 1970.

The following season he beat his own record with a staggering 36 goals in all and won England Under-21 honours. He went on to score four goals in his first three full internationals and was a member of the 1986 England World Cup Squad. He has a total of eight full caps for England.

Kerry can score goals from any position with deadly accuracy. During the 1988-9 season, he continued to chalk up the goals, with a total of 25 in the League.

At the end of 1989-90, he was again the Blues top scorer with a total of 21 League goals.

Kerry had a slow start to 1990-1 but broke his goal duck against Sunderland in the fourth game of the season. At the end of the season, he had scored a total of 10 League goals, bringing his tally for Chelsea to 143.

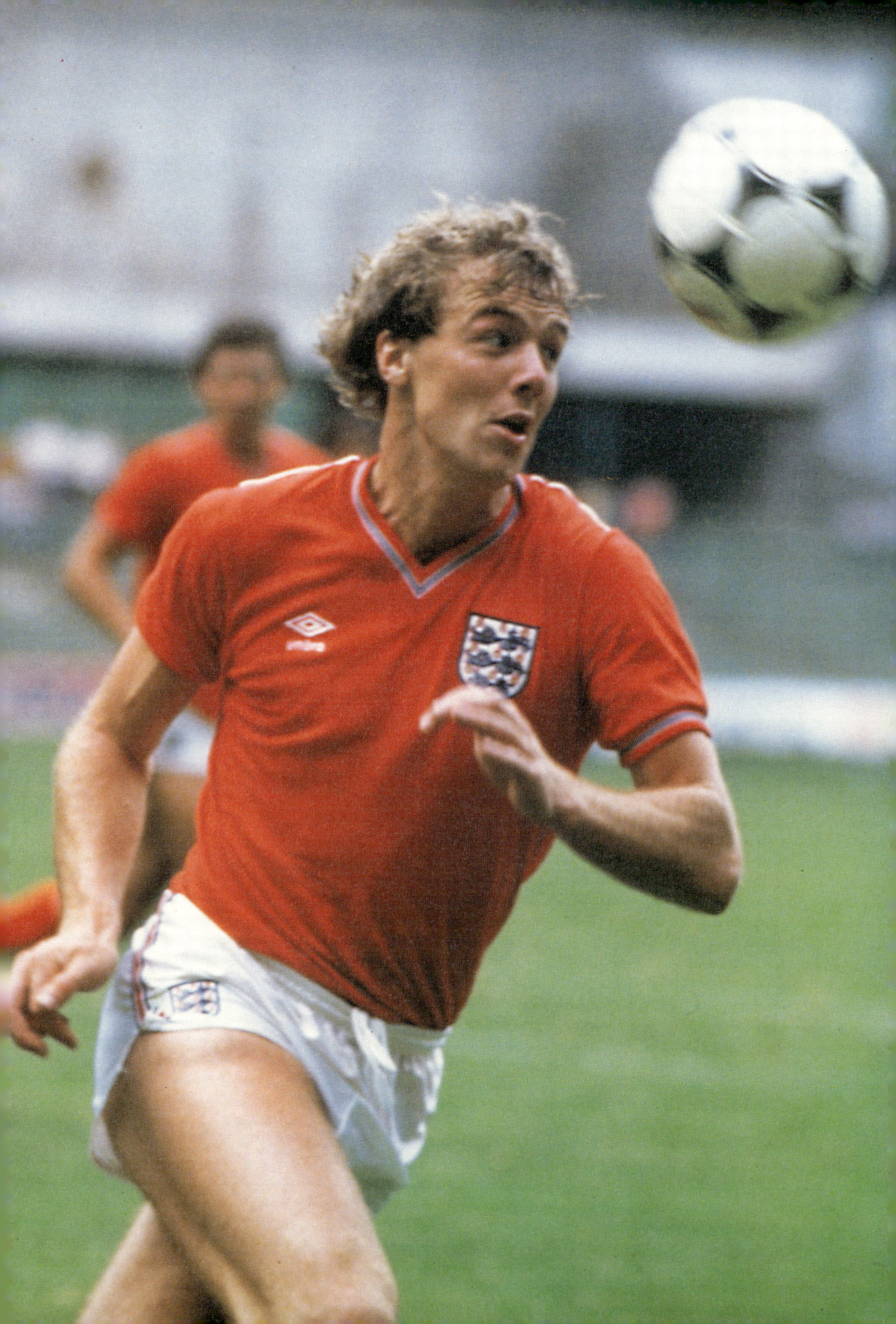

MARK HUGHES

Mark Hughes has been described as one of the most dynamic and exciting strikers in the game today and his extraordinary ability to create goals from seemingly impossible situations has made him a hero at Old Trafford.

Mark was born at Wrexham in North Wales on 1 November 1963. He began playing with Manchester United reserves where he remained for three years as an apprentice. In October 1983 he was given a run-out in the first team as a substitute in a Milk Cup tie against Port Vale. However, it was not until March 1984 that he made his full League debut, when he scored in the 2-0 win over Leicester City.

Within a year Hughes had made a huge impact at Old Trafford, and in the 1984-5 season he was United's top League scorer with 16 goals, including his first hat-trick against Aston Villa on 23 March. He also won his first FA Cup-winners medal when United beat Everton 1-0 after extra-time.

He made his international debut for Wales in May 1984 and scored the only goal of the game, against England, in front of a delighted 'home' crowd at Wrexham. A spectacular goal for his country against Spain in a World Cup qualifier in 1985 drew the attention of several top European clubs, but it was Terry Venables, the Barcelona manager, who secured Hughes' services in a deal reputed to be worth around £2 million. Manchester were outraged at the prospect of losing their brilliant centre-forward to European football, but within two years Hughes was to return to Old Trafford.

Mark's move to Spain was not productive, despite his partnership with Gary Lineker, and he was loaned out to Bayern Munich. His time in Germany was a resounding success and United renewed their interest in the Welshman. In June 1988, he returned to his former club in a £1.8 million deal to play some of the best football of his career. His two years on the continent had sharpened his performance, making him a much more complete player. Hughes earned the ultimate accolade from his fellow professionals when he was voted the PFA's Player of the Year in 1989.

In 1990, he was instrumental in United's FA Cup Final triumph and in 1991 he was again voted PFA Player of the Year.

Hughes' dynamism and flair continue to thrill the Red Devils' supporters and towards the end of the 1990-1 season he had scored a total of 10 League goals and helped United win the European Cup Winners Cup Final against his old club Barcelona with two goals.

Hughes has become a thoroughly accomplished striker, combining his natural talent with excellent control to produce outstanding goals. He has already earned himself a place in Old Trafford legend along with the likes of Denis Law, George Best and Joe Jordan.

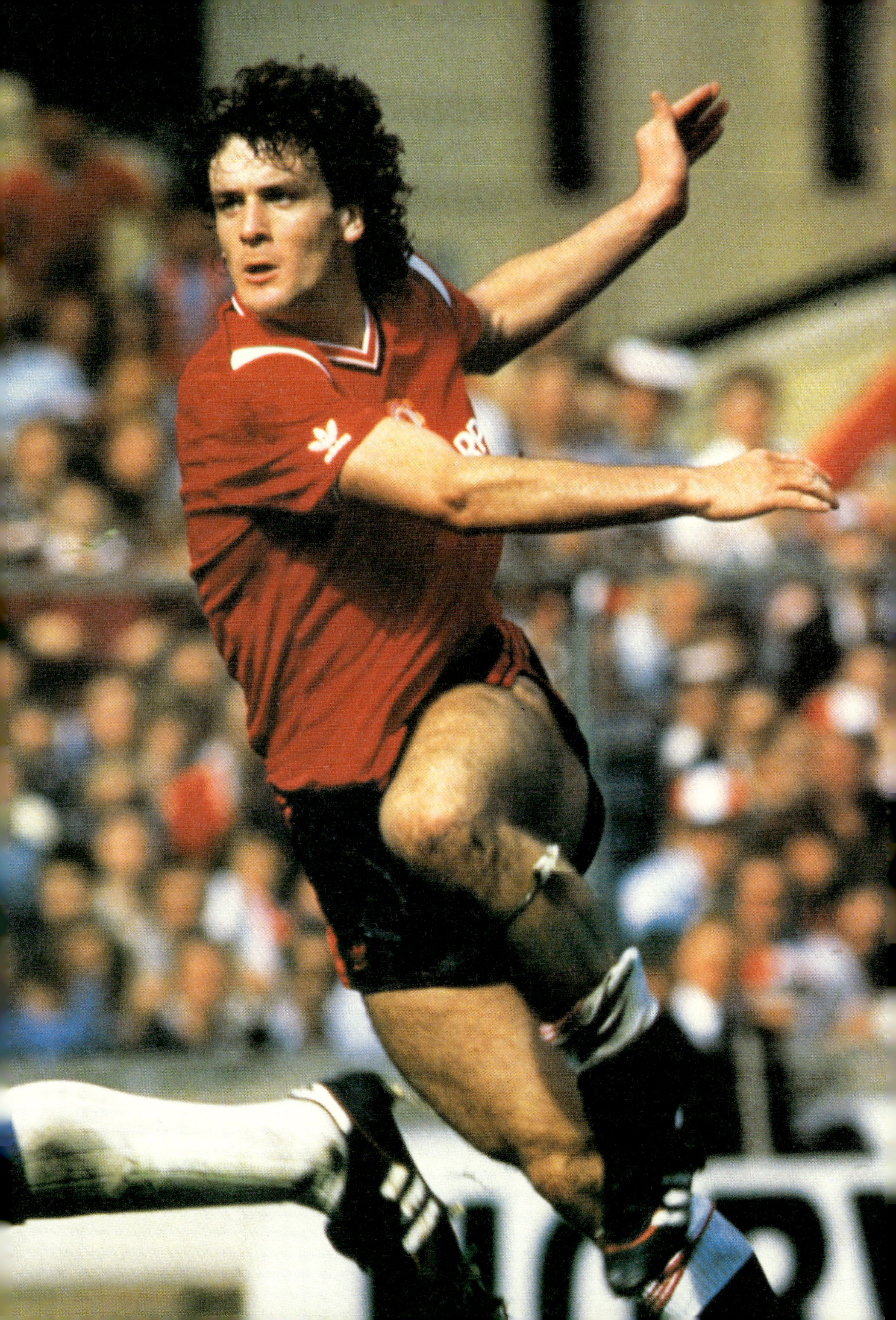

MARCO GABBIADINI

Marco was born in Nottingham on 20 January 1968. His career began with York City where he made his League debut against Bolton on 29 March 1985.

He moved to Sunderland in September 1987, soon after his former manager at York City, Denis Smith, took over at Roker Park and signed him up. Within two years he had scored 50 goals for the club. Only 7 Sunderland players have taken less games to reach the half-century.

Gabbiadini is not just a goalscorer, and is as likely to create a goal as score one. His strength, tenacity and pace make him a formidable opponent for defenders. Marco's own goalscoring heroes are Gary Lineker and Paulo Rossi, Italy's prolific striker of the 1982 World Cup.

He has already won England Under-21 honours and played in the England 'B' team, making his Under-21 debut on 5 June 1989 in a 3-2 defeat by Bulgaria. The 1994 World Cup, when he should be at his peak, may be the time when he realises his full international potential.

Marco's younger brother, Ricardo, is also on Sunderland's books, but not as a regular first team player.

During 1989-90, Marco made 46 League appearances for Sunderland and scored 21 goals.

However, during 1990-1, he had a disappointing season and did not hold his regular first-team place, due to injury problems. He made only 28 appearances and scored 12 goals. His most memorable goal of the season was probably in the opening match, when Sunderland went down 3-2 to Norwich. Marco struck a classic half-volley from 25 yards across goal into the far corner.

Unfortunately, Sunderland were relegated at the end of 1990-1 and Marco will be denied the opportunity of playing against top defenders in the First Division. It will be interesting to watch how his career develops, either with Sunderland or elsewhere, as many First Division clubs must be noting his goalscoring skills.

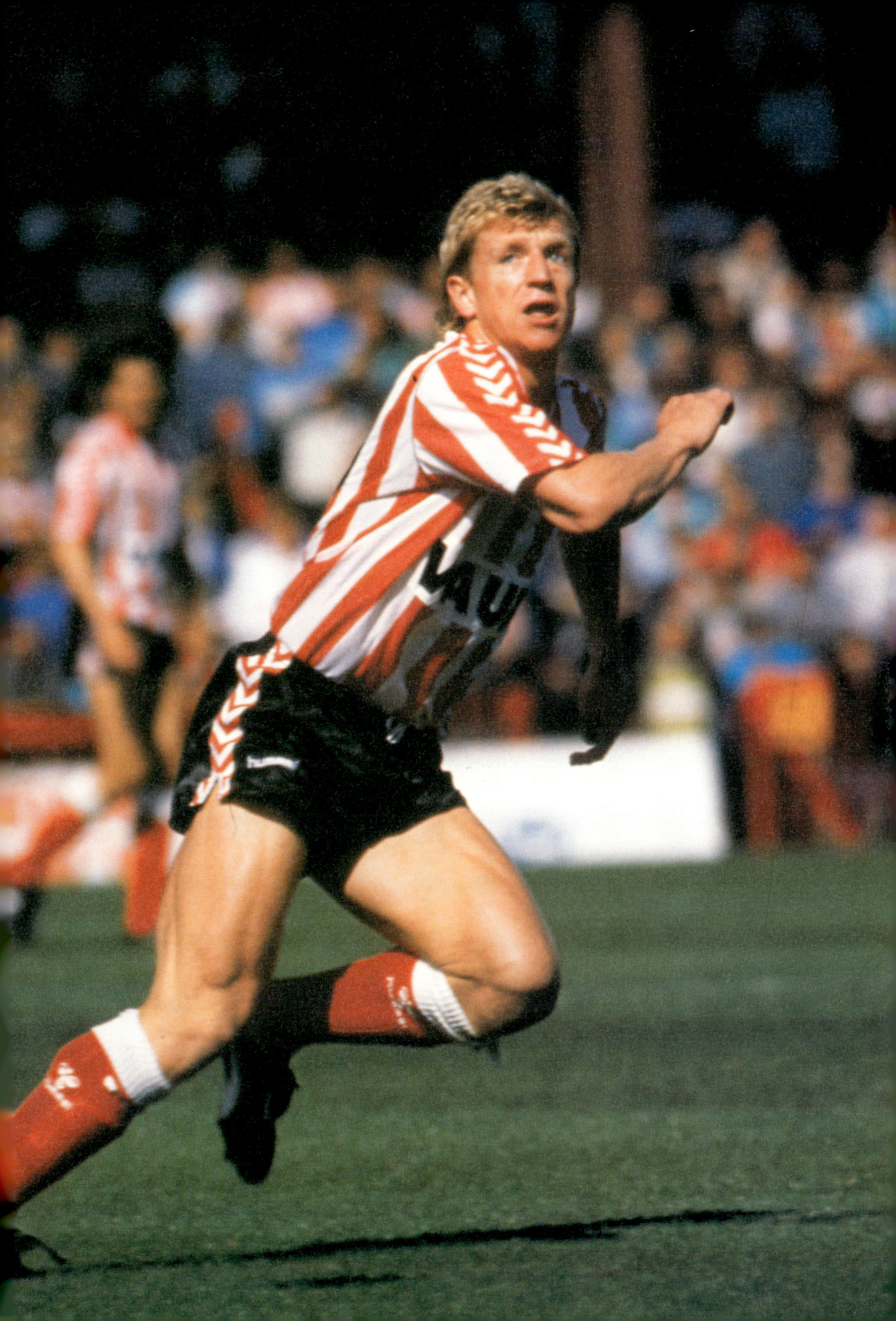

ROY WEGERLE

Roy Wegerle was born on 19 March 1963 in West Germany, but lived in South Africa for many years. He began his soccer career in the USA when he played for Rodney Marsh's Tampa Bay Rowdies in Florida.

He first came to the English League in 1986 and spent two seasons with Chelsea. During that time he had a brief spell on loan with Swindon Town.

In 1988, he moved to Luton Town where he remained until December 1989. He then signed for Queens Park Rangers and became the club's first million pound player.

His best season to date was in 1990-1, when he scored 19 goals in 41 appearances and was voted the QPR Supporters' Club Player of the Year. He has produced some spectacular goals and won the television 'Goal of the Season' award for his terrific solo goal against Leeds United.

A predominantly right-footed player, Roy is at his most lethal within the box, where his skill and accuracy have produced some memorable goals.

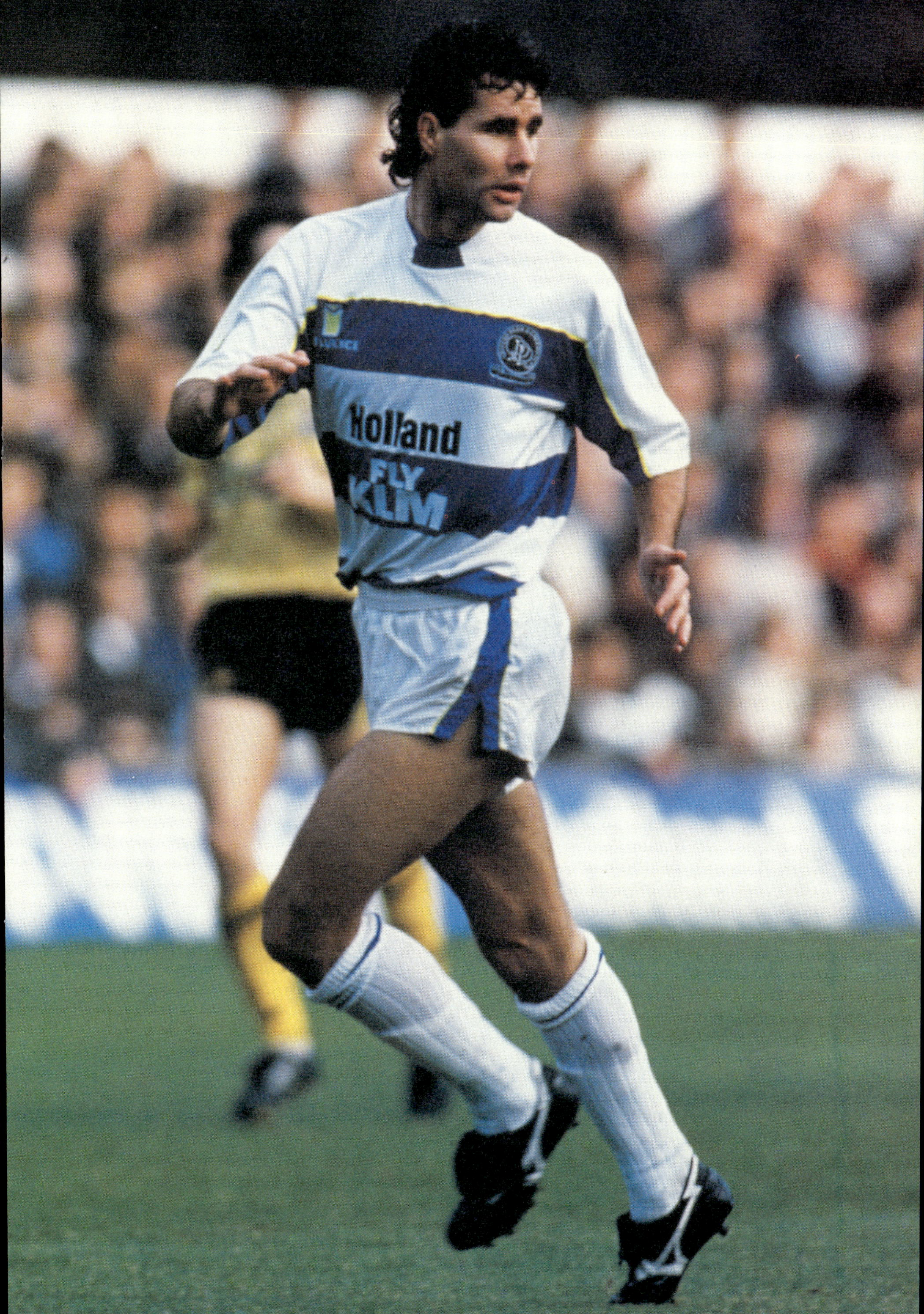
Holland
FLY KLM

MATTHEW LE TISSIER

Matt was born in Guernsey on 14 October 1968 and came to Southampton from Vale Recreation in 1986.

A very exciting player to watch and the Saints' top scorer for two consecutive seasons, Matt looks very likely to be an England star of the future. He has already won England 'B' honours.

He had his most successful season in 1989-90 when he won the PFA Young Player of the Year award and was the club's top scorer with a total of 24 goals. He was also voted Southampton FC Player of the Year.

Last season he consolidated on his success and finished amongst the top ten leading goalscorers in the First Division. He had scored a total of 19 League goals and a total of 23 in all during 1990-1.

Matt has notched up 54 goals in the League since his arrival at Southampton, over five seasons. He has a particularly lethal right foot and rarely misses a chance to score inside the area. He promises to have a dazzling future in the game, both at club and international level.

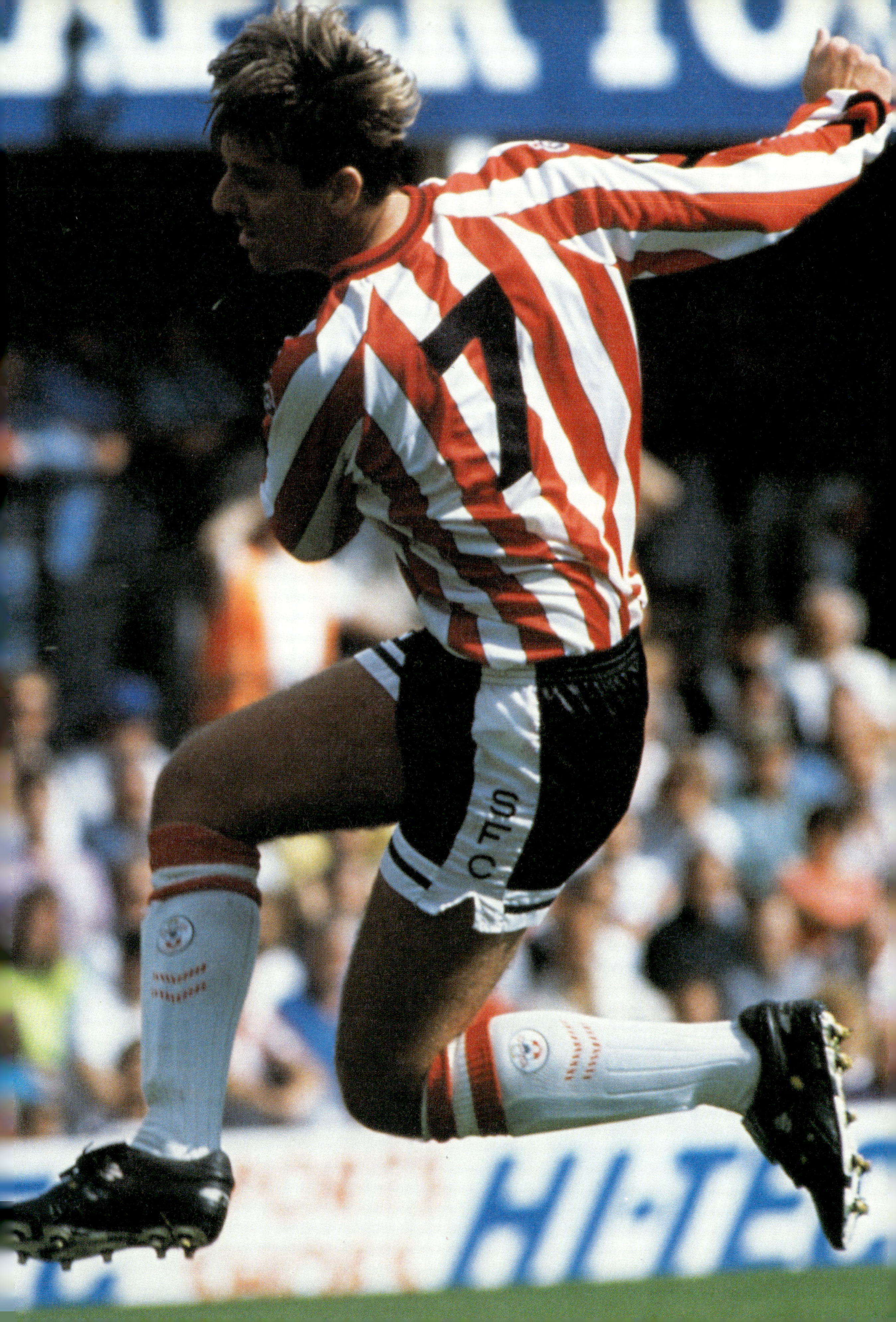
SFC

LEE CHAPMAN

Lee Chapman is one of the most respected strikers in the First Division and played a crucial role in Leed's return to top flight football.

Lee was born in Lincoln on 5 December 1959 and began his career with Stoke City in 1978. At the time he took a year's deferred entry at University, in case his football career did not work out at City. After a brief loan period with Plymouth Argyle, he broke into the Stoke first team and was soon the predominant striker at the Victoria Ground, attracting the attention of many First Division clubs. He remained at Stoke until 1982, having scored 34 League goals in just under 100 matches.

He then went to Arsenal, in what was to be an unhappy move, the Gunners paid £500,000 to secure Chapman's services. At the time this was a high fee for a First Division newcomer and the pressures on him to justify the fee proved immense. After just 16 months, Lee moved to Sunderland, when his former boss at Stoke, Alan Durban, bought him for £200,000. However, after only eight months and 17 appearances, Lee realised it was not working out and his career was finally resurrected with a move to Sheffield Wednesday.

He became a regular scorer for the Owls and during 1987-8 scored 19 goals in 37 appearances. He remained with Wednesday from 1984-8 and chalked up a total of 78 goals, averaging 20 goals a season. His prolific goalscoring led to a move abroad when French club, Niort, expressed an interest in him. However, the deal turned out to be a shambles and Chapman found himself back on the move, this time to Nottingham Forest. After a year and a half with Forest, Lee made the best move of his career to Leeds United.

After his arrival at Elland Road, between 13 January and 5 May 1990 Chapman scored a total of 12 goals, helping United to the Second Division title and promotion.

Chapman consolidated during 1990-1 and with a total of 31 goals in all competitions, he was the top goalscorer in the First Division. He scored a total of 21 League goals, only one behind Arsenal's Alan Smith with 22.

Lee Chapman has matured into a great striker and is currently enjoying the best years of his much travelled career.

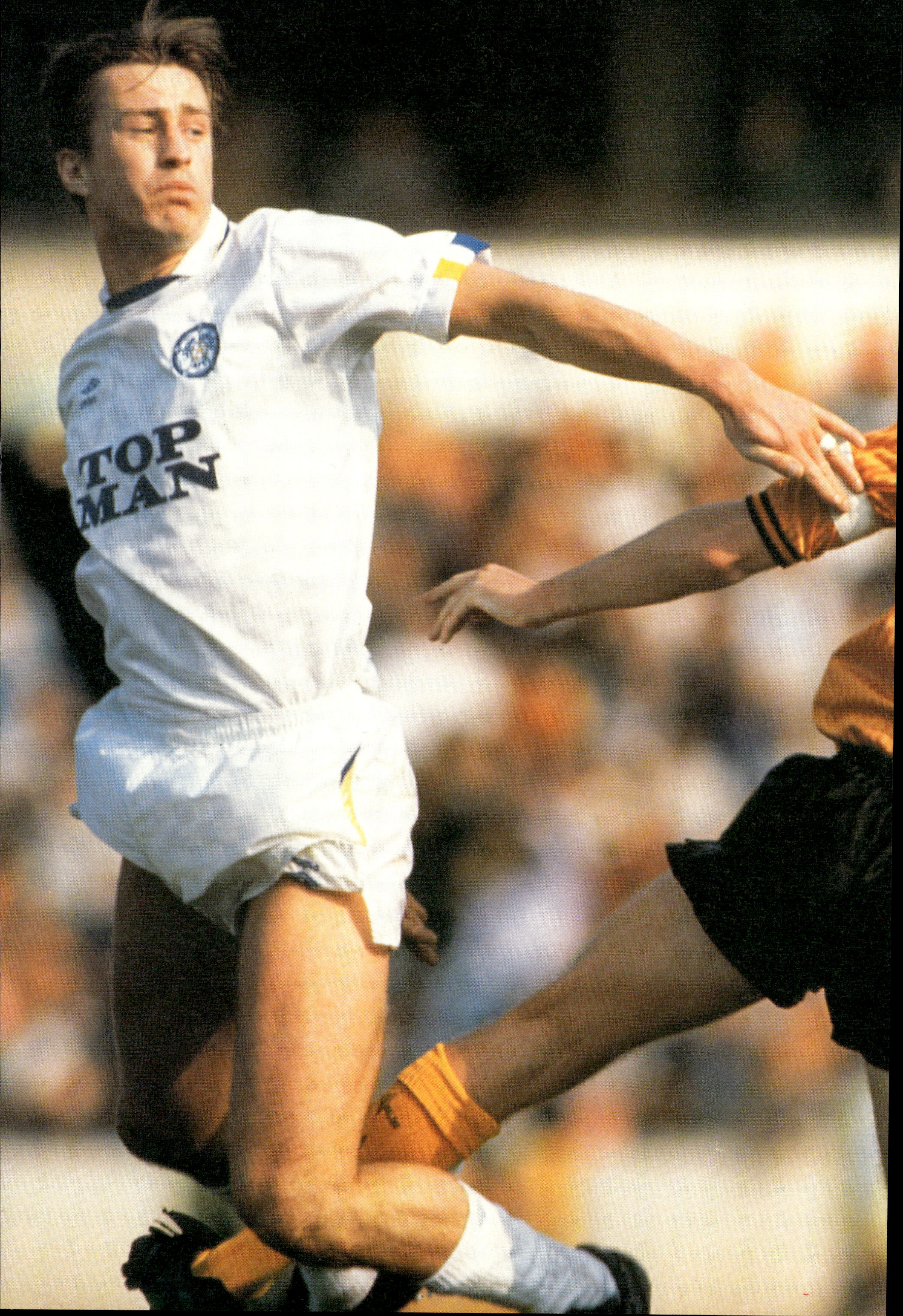
TOP
MAN

BRIAN McCLAIR

McClair's first experience of the English League was an unhappy season at Aston Villa who signed him in 1980-1. Born in Bellhill on 8 December 1963, he returned to his Scottish roots and joined Motherwell the following season.

He soon proved his talent in the Scottish League and Celtic snapped him up in the 1983-4 season. He scored a remarkable 35 League goals and a total of 41 in the last of his four seasons with the Glasgow club.

He returned to English football in 1987, when Manchester United signed him for £850,000. In his first season with United, he netted 24 goals and became the first man since George Best to score over 20 League goals in a season for the Red Devils. In the same season he won his first full cap for Scotland against Luxembourg.

Since then, McClair has gone on to form a lethal partnership with Mark Hughes at United and the pair represent one of the most formidable striking forces in the League. He played a prominent role in United's 1990 FA Cup Final replay against Crystal Palace, when United won 1-0.

He ended the following season in style, with a European Cup-Winners Cup medal, and scored a total of 21 goals, including 13 in the League, making him United's top scorer.

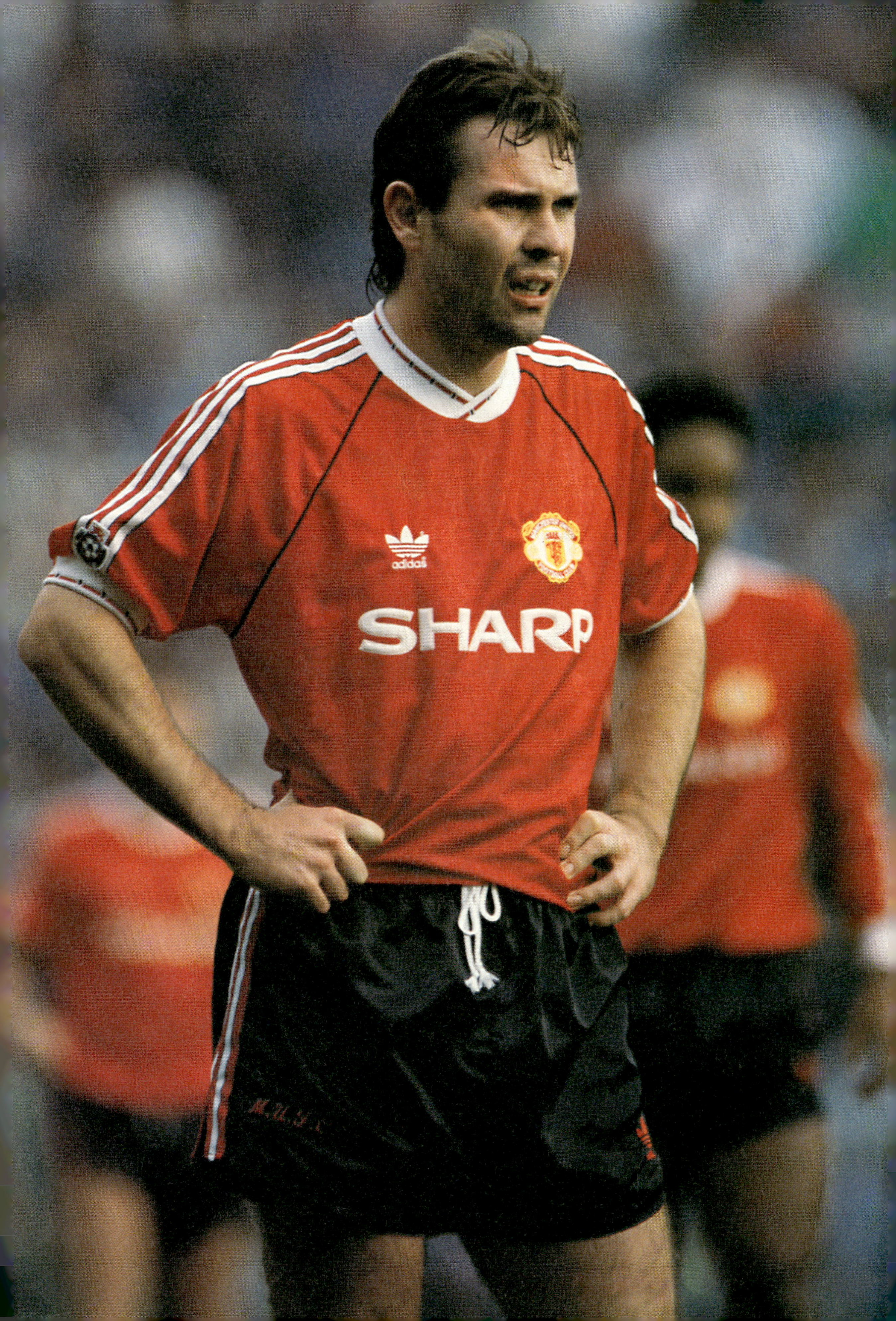
adidas
SHARP

IAN RUSH

Ian Rush is probably the most famous player in Liverpool's star-studded team. He began his career not far from Anfield at Chester in 1978, where he stayed for two seasons.

Ian was born in St. Asaph, North Wales on 20 October 1961 and made his League debut in the Third Division against Sheffield United on 28 April 1979. Yet within a year he was playing top flight football for the mighty Liverpool.

His talent and ability to score goals ensured that the Liverpool scouts spotted him early and signed him up in 1980 for £300,000. Whilst at Chester he netted 14 goals in 34 games and remained at Sealand Road until the end of the season, despite having already signed for Liverpool. Before the move to Anfield, he gained his first full cap for Wales in May 1980.

The usual practice at Liverpool for youngsters to spend a couple of seasons in the reserve team meant that Rush, despite his talent, was no exception. After two seasons, he gained his place in the first team and began his six year reign as 'King of the Kop'.

In 1981-2 he was the Reds' top scorer with 30 goals and in the same year won a Championship medal and scored in the Milk Cup Final win over Spurs.

He consolidated in 1982-3 when he was the club's top scorer and netted four goals in a local derby against Everton. In 1983, he also won further honours with both League Championship and Milk Cup medals.

At the end of the 1983-4 season, Rush scored 32 League goals and went into the record books along with McGuigan and Evans, when he scored five goals in a match against Luton on 29 October 1983, which Liverpool won 6-0!

His success continued for the following two seasons and Liverpool pulled off the double in 1985-6. Again, Rush was the club's top scorer and in the FA Cup Final, he scored two goals in the 3-1 victory against Everton.

During his six years at Anfield, Rush won just about every honour. In a total of 319 appearances he scored 198 goals.

Despite mounting pressure from the Anfield fans to keep Rush at Liverpool, he decided to move to Italian club Juventus, who paid £3,200,000 in what was to be a disastrous move. His prolific goalscoring at Liverpool did not happen in Italy and after an unhappy season Kenny Dalglish brought Rush back to Anfield in a £2,800,000 deal. Both Rush and the fans were delighted.

Although injury problems hindered him initially, he soon found his old form and scored two goals in the 1989 FA Cup Final against Everton, which Liverpool won 3-2. He had again proved himself to be a first class striker and he scored a total of 26 goals, including 18 in the League during 1988-9.

In the 1990-91 season Ian finished amongst the top three leading goalscorers in the First Division, with a total of 26 goals, including 16 in the League.

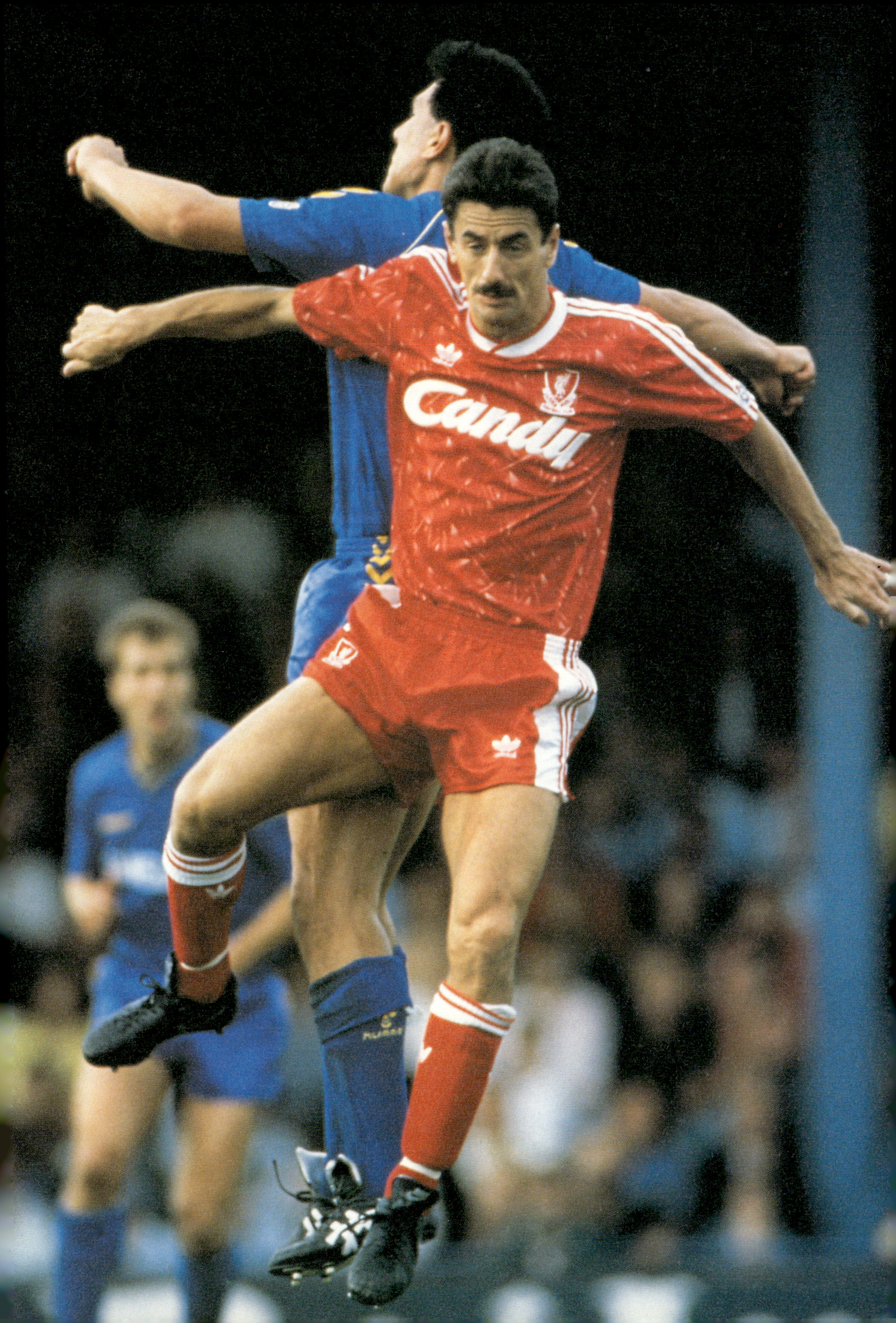
Candy

HUGO SANCHEZ

Hugo Sanchez was born in Mexico City on 11 July 1958. At the age of 20 he made his international debut in the 1978 World Cup. He has since gone on to win numerous caps for his country.

He started his career with Universitario of Mexico City in 1976, but in 1981 moved to Spain, when he was signed by Athletico Madrid for £300,000. In the 1984-5 season, he was the top scorer in the League.

In 1985, he joined local rivals, Real Madrid in a £1.5 million transfer deal. Hugo achieved Many honours with Real, including Spanish League Winners medals from 1986-90 and in 1986 was part of the UEFA Cup-winning side.

He returned to Mexico for the 1986 World Cup to represent the host country. However, he failed to reproduce the match-winning form which had made him a hero at Real. He returned to Spain after a disastrous performance, and his 34 goals helped the club to another League title.

Real's success continued, and in 1989 they won the coveted double with Hugo Sanchez scoring 29 goals over the season.

In 1990-1, Real finished fourth in the Spanish First Division League and although Hugo was not the top goalscorer, he finished amongst the top ten with 12 goals.

MARCO VAN BASTEN

Marco was born in Utrecht on 31 October 1964 and began playing with little known Elinwijik, but soon gained a reputation and was signed by the mighty Ajax in 1981 when he was just 17.

During his five year stay at Ajax he won numerous honours. He scored 128 goals and won Dutch League Championship medals in 1982, 1983 and 1985. He won the coveted Adidas Golden Boot Award in 1986, with a total of 37 goals.

Shortly before moving to AC Milan in a £3.3 million transfer in 1987, Marco scored the only goal in the European Cup Winners' Cup Final against Lokomotiv Leipzig to win Ajax the Cup.

Unfortunately, injuries kept Marco on the bench for most of the 1987-8 season, but amazingly, he hit peak form for the European Championships in West Germany. He was top scorer with five goals, including a hat trick against England, and Holland won the tournament. His performance also earned him the European Footballer of the Year award for 1988.

The following season Marco was back on form for his club and helped AC Milan to success in the European Cup in 1989. They beat Steaua Bucharest 4-0, with Marco scoring twice. He was later voted European Footballer of the Year for a second successive season.

In the 1990 World Cup van Basten played in all four of Holland's matches, but did not score. During the 1990-1 season, van Basten scored 11 League goals and AC Milan finished second in the League, just behind Sampdoria, by a three point margin.

JURGEN KLINSMANN

Germany's Jurgen Klinsmann first gained fame in 1988, when he was voted West Germany's Footballer of the Year and was the country's leading scorer with 19 goals. In the same year he emerged as the star player in his country's European Championship team. Klinsmann had made his mark on the international scene. He has since won 30 caps and scored nine goals for his country.

He was born on 30 July 1964 and began his career with Stuttgart Kickers. He then moved to VFB Stuttgart, before leaving the German League to join Internazionale.

In the 1990 World Cup in Italy, Klinsmann gave some tremendous individual performances and was a key player in the victorious German side. He played in all seven matches and scored three goals, his first in the Germans' 4-1 win over Yugoslavia. He scored against the United Arab Emirates and in the second round he got one of Germany's goals in their 2-1 defeat of Holland. He returned to the Italian League for another successful season with Internazionale and notched up a total of 14 League goals during the 1990-1 season.

However, despite his great talent and prolific goalscoring, Klinsmann has only ever won one medal at club level with Internazionale in the 1991 UEFA Cup Final against AC Roma.

GIANLUCA VIALLI

Talented Italian striker, Vialli, has made a remarkable recovery during the 1990-1 season, after a disappointing World Cup.

During the World Cup, 'Luca' made three appearances but did not score, much to the despair of the Italian fans. After the disappointment of Italia '90, he was excluded from the national side, but his recent club form has ensured his return to the Italian team.

Vialli finished the 1990-1 season with a total of 19 League goals, making him the country's top scorer and helping Sampdoria to the Serie A Title. Not so long ago Sampdoria were not rated against Italy's top clubs, Napoli, AC Milan, Internazionale and AC Roma. However, away victories have confirmed the club's new status and the striking partnership of Vialli and Mancini has proved lethal against the best opposition.

'Luca's revival as a top striker will go a long way to securing his place in the national side in the forthcoming 1992 European Championship.

LOTHAR MATTHAUS

German captain, Lothar Matthaus, has gained 80 caps for his country and is one of the most formidable strikers in Europe.

In the 1990 World Cup, Matthaus played in all seven games and scored four goals, including the only goal against Czechoslovakia in the quarter finals, which he took from the penalty spot. His immense contribution undoubtedly helped the German team to World Cup victory.

At club level, he had a tremendous season with Internazionale in 1990-1 and finished the second highest scorer in the League with 16 goals. Inter also won the UEFA Cup, their first European trophy for 26 years, though much controversy surrounded the defensive tactics of Inter's coach, Trappatoni, in the 2-1 aggregate win against Roma. After Matthaus voiced his discontent with the club, Real Madrid are reported to be interested in the goal-getting German and it looks likely that he will be joining the Spanish side at the beginning of 1991-2.

ROBERTO BAGGIO

Juventus have always been well represented in the best Italian national teams, and the 1990 World Cup was no exception, with sensational striker, Roberto Baggio delighting the host nations supporters.

Baggio joined Juventus for a staggering £7.7 million from Florentina in 1990, though over the years the Turin club has gained a reputation for spending many millions on top players.

During Italia '90, Baggio produced one of the finest individual goals of the tournament, when he played a one-two with Giannini from the half-way line and blitzed through the defence to score in spectacular style, in the first-round match against Czechoslovakia. He scored once more against England in the play-off for third place when Italy won 2-1.

During the 1990-1 season, Juventus finished seventh in the League and despite Baggio's 14 goals, are out of European competition next season for the first time in 28 years.